# CAN'T SEE THE WOOD FOR THE TREES?

"The Landscaping Your Life process presented in the book shows us how the metaphors we use to describe our lives might be initially disempowering but then go on to stimulate creative ways out of our mental traps."
— Geoff Roberts, catalyst at Hidden Resources

"Landscaping Your Life is a brilliant approach, heartily recommended. Alison has extraordinary energy and an almost spooky sense of where people are and what they need. I have learned/worked/played alongside Alison for more than a decade and found her insights always useful."
— Ruth Wallsgrove, management consultant

"Alison and I first had the discussion about using metaphors to solve a challenge I was facing in a Warsaw restaurant a few years ago. At the time I thought, 'What? Give me more wine…this is uncomfortable'. Then I persisted and the answer presented itself, by using the metaphor, and I was converted."
— Sara Walsh Evans, managing director at The Respectory

"There is nothing more invigorating than taking a step back and being challenged to view life with a different perspective. Whether it is seeing the wood for the trees, stepping out of a rut or not burying your head in the sand…all techniques outlined in this book have helped me face life head on!"
— Cara Murphy, commercial contract and supplier management, Mountain View Consulting

"Alison is one of the best coaches I have ever had the pleasure of working with (and I've worked with a few!). She has a highly practical nature and combines it with strong intuition and unconventional tools to guide you to find insights and answers to specific challenges... As with any transformational coaching, you need to be prepared to take responsibility for personal change and get out of your comfort zone to find the answers you need, but Alison makes this easy with her approach."

— Mel Sherwood, author of *The Authority Guide to Pitching Your Business*

"I told Alison I knew I was making a bit of a mountain out of a molehill for an issue I had, and even though I knew this, I was still stuck. She asked me questions about it, so I looked at my metaphor for the problem in a different light. She made me see that how I saw the problem was affecting my ability to do something about it."

— Caroline Johnstone, author of *An Introduction to the Magic of Journaling*

"Alison always hits the nail on the head when it comes to steering me in the right direction, whether personally or for a business issue. She is great to work with and a very positive person. I would recommend her whether you just need more clarity in your life or if you are looking for a whole new direction."

— Brian Wood, owner of the Message Collective

"It's too easy to get caught up in the content of a challenge we're facing. That is, 'she said this, and I said that', and before we know it all we've done is spent hours talking ourselves into justifying why we're stuck and why we can't do anything about it. With Alison as my guide, the use of landscapes as metaphors for issues I'm facing has allowed me to observe the situation afresh without the oughts, shoulds and can'ts getting in the way. By noticing a new path, turning a real or metaphorical corner, stepping out of a rut, or cutting down some imaginary trees, solutions have emerged. More importantly, action plans developed and steps taken in a new direction."

— Sufiya Gillespie, coaching client

# CAN'T SEE THE WOOD FOR THE TREES?

## LANDSCAPING YOUR LIFE TO GET BACK ON TRACK

ALISON SMITH

*f* FINDHORN PRESS

Findhorn Press
One Park Street
Rochester, Vermont 05767
www.findhornpress.com

Findhorn Press is a division of Inner Traditions International

**Disclaimer**
The information in this book is given in good faith and intended for information
only. Neither author nor publisher can be held liable by any person for any loss or
damage whatsoever which may arise from the use of this book or any of the
information therein. All clients names used in this book have been changed for
reasons of confidentiality.

A CIP record for this title is available from the Library of Congress

ISBN 978-1-84409-749-4 (print)
ISBN 978-1-84409-765-4 (ebook)

Printed and bound in the United States by Versa Press, Inc.

10 9 8 7 6 5 4 3 2 1

Edited by Jacqui Lewis
Text design and layout by Geoff Green Book Design
This book was typeset in adobe Caslon
Artwork by Alison Smith

To send correspondence to the author of this book, mail a first-class letter to the
author c/o Inner Traditions • Bear & Company, One Park Street, Rochester, VT
05767, USA and we will forward the communication, or contact the author directly
at **www.landscapingyourlife.co.uk**

TO MUM AND DAD
WITH LOVE X

# CONTENTS

# INTRODUCTION

Sometimes when we're invited to consider what's holding us back, we can find it very easy to be defensive. To jump straight in to justify our current actions, to explain why what we're doing is right. To deny the rightness of the advice of others and hold on to our own beliefs, despite those beliefs contributing to our current predicament.

Obviously, this defensiveness is not a helpful behaviour when we wish to release the current stuck situation and get back on track, headed towards a new more desirable outcome.

Perhaps my ease in recognizing this defensiveness in others is due to my own relationship with this behaviour. I'm on first-name terms with it, and I'm particularly defensive when hearing feedback about what changes I may need to think about making. I don't want to see evidence that I might be wrong, or that I have failed in the past. I want to get there first, to make changes based on my own say-so and definitely not on someone else's.

It's as if my "no one is going to tell me what to do – la-la-la" inner voice is turned up so loud I can hear nothing else, even at times deafening me to my own advice.

This defensiveness is there irrespective of whether those changes are related to my health, fitness, relationships, work or life more generally, and irrespective of my own personal level of expertise on the matter. Gavin, my personal trainer, can certainly testify to having to walk the tightrope I've laid down to keep me fit and healthy, despite my controlling behaviour making his job much harder, and I suspect this frustrates him greatly. (Sorry Gavin).

Perhaps my own resistance to being told what to do is why metaphors became such a go-to tool in my own personal development. Their efficacy and success for me personally meant that I could simply use and develop them as I worked with others who are stuck and wanting desperately to find a way of getting back on track.

Metaphors get me back on track because they bypass the resistance I've put up to being told what to do. That is, I don't have to deal with my resistance and need for control every time change is needed. It's as if the language of metaphor talks directly to the more creative part of my brain, without needing to worry the more logical part that wants to retain control at all times. The creative and perhaps more subconscious part of me hears the message, and takes appropriate action.

Instead of la-la-la we have ah-ha!

Very soon after I started to use metaphors in coaching others to get back on track, I realized nature provided a means of exploring metaphors not just in our minds but also in reality, resulting in even more powerful ah-ha's.

I called the process of using nature as a metaphor for our lives Landscaping Your Life.

By way of explanation, let me start by applying Landscaping Your Life to my need for control.

## "Trying to control your life is like trying to control the weather"

Please note: as I'm not a meteorologist, some of the following assumptions may be factually incorrect. In some respect, while factual data may add something to my analysis, it's more important for me to notice what I notice about the weather and to apply that insight to my need for control.

Here's what I might observe as a reflection on that statement.

- Weather is very changeable – (here in Scotland anyway – it's certainly never static!).
- Changes in weather are determined by a combination of factors – air pressure, wind direction and speed, moisture in the air, height above sea level, time of year/day, sun, cloud, time of day.

- Weather is never the same on any day in any location – it's in a constant state of flux.
- Weather is the outcome of a closed system with a constant need to get back to equilibrium.
- The greater differential between the current weather and equilibrium there is, the higher the potential for "bigger", more violent weather.
- No control is needed – just an acceptance of how the world works and an allowing of the inevitable outcome so that equilibrium can be found.
- The only control we have over the weather is to wear the appropriate clothing so that we're dry when it's wet, protected when it's sunny and secure when it's windy.
- Another aspect of control with respect to the weather is measuring it – perhaps not as simplistically as with a weather vane, but using measurements that enable forecasters to provide 24, 48, 72-hour forecasts and beyond. This is not control as such, but the advance warning means we can be more prepared for what happens, rather than be surprised.

During a full Landscaping Your Life coaching session we might spend some time exploring other aspects of weather – how it differs according to longitude and latitude, warm weather, hot, dry, humid, wet, violent, calm, and so on.

From this very simple exploration of weather the biggest insight for me is that we can't control the weather, only forecast and adequately prepare for it and then manage the outcome. Trying to control the weather is much like trying to make it the same time of day, or the same time of year, all the time. That's not how the world works, and trying to control it drains and wastes energy that could be put to much better use.

As I reflect on how this relates to my life I realize it's impossible to try to control all aspects of life. All I can do is put processes in place to provide me with data so that I can adapt more easily to the changing world around me. I might have come to this realization without use of the weather metaphor, but I find it easier to accept, assimilate and act upon it when shared via the metaphor. It's as if my resistance to change is relaxed as I am able to laugh at my own belief in controlling the uncontrollable.

Yes, I did think I could control my life – and realizing that it was like trying to control the weather has enabled me to understand the futility of my behaviour.

One other insight from the weather was to ensure I have a range of clothes to choose from that keep me safe, warm and dry – no matter what weather is thrown at me! Which reminds me of my experience sitting on a bus in the pitch dark in the middle of Iceland with 40 other people.

It was below zero outside and we were all wrapped up in hats, scarves, gloves, well-insulated boots and many, many layers in the hope of keeping ourselves warm despite the weather. We were, however, still very cold. It was 11 p.m. and thoughts of a warm bed were not far away as we scanned the sky for a treasure we'd all dreamt about for some time.

We were hunting the Northern Lights – the aurora borealis.

Like anything related to the weather and nature, aurora hunting isn't quite as simple as you might think, even with the best forecasting data to hand. We'd been out hunting for five hours the night before, and seen nothing. Tonight was different, and I had great hopes that we'd achieve our goal.

While we moved from location to location the guide told us stories about Iceland, and Icelandic history. One comment caught my attention, and made me as excited as I would be when we did eventually see the magnificent aurora a little later that night.

"In Iceland there's a saying: if you can't see the wood for the trees – stand up."

Not only a reminder that the sayings we use when we're stuck often have nature metaphors contained within them, but also a reminder that these sayings translate across languages.

It's as if metaphor transcends language, providing meaning at a deeper level.

Let's explore the Icelandic saying a little more – if you couldn't see the wood for the trees in Iceland and stood up, you'd be able to see over the top of them, because the native trees just don't grow very tall. Although they are in fact real trees, they look more like bushes; the environment just makes it difficult for them to grow. Apparently trees in the Arctic are even smaller!

If I now apply this saying to a real-life situation I can't see the wood for the trees about, such as one many people face regularly – what to do about a number of career choices – then observations may include:

- Stand up and back from the situation, and compare these career options from a neutral position.
- Remember that Icelandic trees are small as a result of the lack of the right conditions for growth. We may therefore wish to consider what the right conditions are for us to personally flourish in a career or job.
- Notice that if a tree can look like a shrub, then looks can be deceiving; go and check out the credentials of all the career options.
- Observe that non-native trees flourish better, and consider the culture of the organizations being considered.

And that's just the insights that can be obtained from one observation about what to do when you can't see the wood for the trees when out in nature.

Other insights that might appear if we go for a walk in a wood, perhaps even a large wood, include:

- Get your map out – which might be about you reminding yourself where you've wanted to go in your career – i.e., what values need to be met, what life balance have you wanted, what do you enjoy, what are you good at, what do you get excited about at work, and so on.
- Chop some of the trees down – ask yourself if all the options are of equal interest or if you can use your "must have" rather than "want to have" criteria to whittle the number of options down.
- Look for paths – are some of the choices easier to take than others? What else has to be in place for each of the options to

> work (moving home, childcare arrangements, finishing a course, looking after parents, travelling, and so on)?.
> • Wait till winter comes, and the trees are easier to see due to the lack of leaves – does the decision have to be made today or can it wait until you have more clarity about what to do?

Thinking of your current issue from a metaphorical position means you no longer sit there, like a rabbit in the headlights, dazzled by the options. Instead, your mind is freed to look for different perspectives from nature's point of view.

The above suggestions may sound like obvious solutions, but not if we are using "Can't see the wood for the trees" about the situation. If we're using this saying, which means we're stuck, we *are* stuck, and don't know what to do. If we knew what to do, we wouldn't be using the saying.

I think that may need saying again – if you're using the saying then at some level you're stuck, and don't know what to do, and so your options do not seem obvious at all!

The genius of the Landscaping Your Life process outlined in this book lies in the fact that it uses each saying to describe the situation and then to identify opportunities.

I get very excited every time I hear myself say that the solution and opportunities can also be found in the saying we're using.

Yes, you read right – we're using the language that describes the stuck situation to find the answer.

How fabulous is that?

It's not even the language as much as the landscape contained within our description of the situation.

Which means:

> • If you're stuck in a rut, you'll find the solution in the rut.
> • If you're up the creek without a paddle, the options available are the same as those for how to get out of the creek, and may or may not include finding a paddle.

In other words, you need to stop making mountains from the mole-hills.

- If you're like a fish out of water, you definitely need to get back in the water.
- If you've got your head in the sand the one thing you need to do is take it out of the sand.
- If you're out on a limb you either need to step back on the limb, or let go of the limb.
- If you're treading water, you need to find a way of stopping doing that.
- If you've missed the tide you need to remember there's another tide in less than 13 hours.

That's what this book is all about – taking these sayings that we use to describe being stuck, and using the sayings themselves to get unstuck.

Let's rewind a little.

In the coaching I do my area of expertise has always been helping people get unstuck. Once they're back on track I'm not the coach to stay around and hold their hand as they continue on their way. My joy comes from getting others unstuck – which is what this book is all about. It's why I'm very good at it – it's what I've been helping people to do for nearly 20 years.

The premise of the book is that the solution for any state of stuckness is achieved by first accepting a number of beliefs:

- The language you use provides clues to how you're perceiving the current situation.
- You know the answer – even if currently unconsciously.
- Exploring the metaphors contained within your language allows your subconscious to communicate to your conscious awareness.
- Using metaphor reduces resistance and the barriers you put up to change.

When we say we're stuck in a rut, out on a limb or going round in circles, we're providing clues about how we're currently relating to the current situation, and there's a part of us that does know the solution.

I'll write that again.

Yes, a part of you already knows the solution.

Yes, YOU – not me.

Not your significant other.

Not your colleagues.

Not your coach.

Not your friends.

Although they may all be able to support you.

Yes, YOU. You know how to get back on track. You just need to access and listen to the part of you that knows, rather than the part of you that wants to keep your head buried in the sand, or the part of you that quite likes being lost in the trees unable to see the wood, or prefers to be a fish that stays safe in its small bowl, rather than take the risk of jumping to the bigger one.

The question then becomes: how do we access the parts of us that know the answer, but are obviously hiding from us?

The language we use often gives us a clue as to where the solution might lie.

The language of metaphor even more so – after all, if a picture paints a thousand words then a metaphor paints a thousand pictures. In other words, a metaphor provides a million words that, I would contend, will undoubtedly have the solution contained within them.

To give you a sense of this let's explore a familiar metaphor used for achieving our goals.

Mountains are a great metaphor used for achievement. Success is often depicted as someone standing at the top of a mountain next to a flag, or problems we encounter are described as uphill struggles; and when we're making something of nothing we're accused of making mountains out of molehills.

The reason for the mountain metaphor is simple – climbing a mountain requires many of the same activities and attributes as achieving anything in life.

- Know where you are (A).
- Know where you're headed (B).
- Know why it's important for you to get from A to B.
- Know what you need to do to get from A to B.
- Plan the route, and prepare accordingly.
- Take the first step.
- Check progress towards your goal, and amend plan accordingly (i.e., make those course corrections).

Most failures can certainly be found to lie in one of these areas – whether climbing mountains in reality, or trying to reach another goal.

When walking up real mountains (the really big snow-capped ones) you don't often get to the top in one go. There are many "false" mountaintops along the way. You think you're there when you're not, because this is just the first of many, many mini-summits.

Isn't that a lot like life? Where there are many mini-summits between us and our goals, and they are the only thing stopping us getting to our goal.

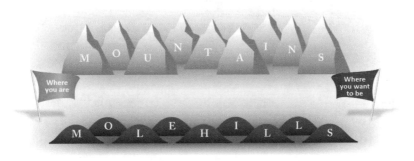

The process outlined in this book makes these mini-summits (mountains along the way) into manageable molehills. The mountains to be reduced in size are found in the sayings we use to describe how we're feeling.

The molehills are the antidote, and while the MOLEHILLS acronym identifies the actual steps to be taken in real life, we're going to be looking for the solution in the metaphor of the mountains – i.e., if you feel like a fish out of water, continuing to use the saying/metaphor to provide insight will be helpful, and thinking like a fish might just provide you with insight! (You'll find more on how to do that later.)

The process to be covered in this book therefore covers the following mountains or sayings and has the MOLEHILLS outlined as antidotes:

| | The Mountains<br>Why you're stuck<br>What's stopping you | The Molehills<br>The Antidote<br>The Action | What the molehill<br>helps you to do |
|---|---|---|---|
| M | Stuck in a rut | **M**otivation | To get out of bed and take action<br>To be inspired and excited<br>To make changes |
| O | Can't see the wood for the trees | **O**utcome | To know what you're headed towards (B) |
| L | Up the creek without a paddle | **L**ife as it is now (what we're leaving behind) | To know where you are now (A) |
| E | Like a fish out of water | **E**motional intelligence | To understand yourself and manage your state |
| H | Head in the sand | **H**ead out of the sand | To take personal responsibility for your life |
| I | Out on a limb | **I**nterference removed | To understand and remove what's holding you back |
| LL | Going round in circles | **L**ongitude and **L**atitude | To develop the route for getting from A to B |
| S | Missed the tide | **S**tart | To take the first step |

What this process suggests is that, if you're stuck, it's one of the above "mountains" that will be what's stopping you.

The process of identifying your mountains, and using the antidote molehills, can be achieved in many different ways.

Lots of books have been written about each of the molehills. If you're stuck in a rut, therefore, you could go and read a book about motivation, or watch a TED talk to be inspired. Or, when you feel like a fish out of water, listen to a Daniel Goleman talk about emotional intelligence.

I want to stick with the mountains and use the sayings we use when we're stuck to help make the process even easier. After all, if the basic construct of the book is making molehills from the mountains, this then means:

- Stepping out of the rut
- Being the fish back in water
- Paddling out of the creek
- Taking your head out of the sand
- Going with the flow
- Being able to see the wood
- Catching the tide

Some of you may want to read more about why I'm using sayings, why I'm using nature, why I think such metaphors work and a bit more about the theory behind the process. In which case do jump ahead to chapters 1–4.

Others of you will just want to try out the Landscaping Your Life process – if so, each chapter is self-contained, with instructions for how to use it. Go to Part 2 and jump straight to a saying that best describes how you're feeling at the moment, giving it a score from 1 to 10 on your level of stuckness in relation to the situation where 0 is stuck and 10 is on track.

## How to Use the Book

The steps outlined in each chapter are in an order that makes some semblance of sense. You can think of an issue you'd like insight on and read the book sequentially, making a note of any insights or actions along the way. It will walk you through the process, from understanding why change is needed to understanding more about the goal, and what needs to take place to make it a reality. If you've been stuck for some time, and that stuckness has perhaps spread out into a number of areas of your life, I'd also recommend reading all the chapters about the sayings in sequence.

One of the mountains, or sayings, however, may resonate more with how you're feeling at this moment in time – in which case why not jump straight into that chapter and notice what you notice. After first reading Chapter 3, that is, which provides more guidance about the process.

Similarly, one of the molehills may resonate – in which case, again, why not go to the chapter on its corresponding mountain and see what you discover about the situation in hand.
Remember:

- The aim is to get back on track – unstuck and back into the flow.
- A part of you does know what to do.
- Currently it's quite likely that use of the saying is keeping you stuck.

In the past, the way we've used these sayings will have certainly kept us stuck, i.e., we can't see a solution because we're using the normal meaning of the saying. We're believing that if we're in a rut we can't get out of it, or that if we're the fish out of water we're doomed to just keep gasping for air. Not surprising then that we feel stuck! It's as if the saying is keeping us stuck in a loop, with no ability to flex and change the situation. The Landscaping Your Life process jars us out of the loop into a different route to finding an answer.

This process turns everything on its head, and asks us to consider what would happen if the saying did actually contain the solution. If I were a fish out of water, what would the fish do? Or if I were a fish that was going to be out of water what would I, as the fish, do? How would I react?

Yes, it may feel a little odd (or downright weird), but trust yourself enough to know that if the saying resonates with how you're feeling in this moment, then it is the right saying for you at this point and you can continue to use it to find the solution.

Every reader will relate to a saying differently, and have a unique landscape that represents it or allows them to explore what that means for them. This book therefore can only act as a guide, and provide some overarching questions that may help you explore the situation, get insight and potentially find resolution.

In workshops using this process we spend a lot of time just exploring the sayings. To allow each participant to understand the process and get it into their muscle memory. To give them the confidence to know that there is no right or wrong, that everyone's journey through their landscape and to clarity about their intention will be different.

The language throughout the book, therefore, is deliberately permissive, to allow you to explore a landscape in a way that makes perfect sense to you. Even if not one other person would ever look at it the same way as you do. Of course, in group settings there is a power to be found when everyone is using the same saying. Ten people in a room all up the creek without a paddle enables us to see the situation from other perspectives.

I remember on one occasion being very resistant to resolving a situation, and the clarity I found from observing someone else share their journey and insights. It was as if she'd gone on that journey for me. Having time to observe someone else gave me the space and time to make an internal shift, which I'd been unable to do on my own. Suddenly the ah-ha that had been eluding me was apparent.

The best way to describe it is to say that currently you can't see the solution, and you know, for example, that it's like being up the creek without a paddle. There is a part of you that knows how these two are related, otherwise how else would you be able to agree that yes, that is how you feel? That's why, when you find a solution within the metaphor, the part of you that understands the relationship between the two will find a solution in real life too.

It may not be immediately clear, but overnight or in the morning when you wake or when meditating, an insight may come and you will know that's what you need to do in the current situation.

If the questions at the start of each chapter don't help enough, then read my explanation, which should provide further insight or perspective on the current situation and, more importantly, what action you need to take to get moving.

The more you can explore these landscapes on your own, the better. As soon as you start listening to my questions, they might potentially change your relationship to the metaphor. For example, I might ask what time of day it is in the image you have of the landscape, and inadvertently change your perception of the situation, not necessarily for the best.

Remember, the saying is how your brain is representing the current situation. You have two options – try to solve it by considering the current situation in real life, or see what additional insight is gleaned from exploring the metaphor. Remember that to use the metaphor is to access one million words, and is therefore a very rich source of potential for you.

A word of warning. The process can be used time and time again, for varying states of stuckness, and applied to any situation in your life. If you visit a saying for a second time, remember that the situation you're applying it to is different and therefore so may be the solution. Answer the questions, and notice what difference there is this time.

If you find yourself repeatedly returning to a specific saying, you may want to consider what conclusion you can draw from that. Does the saying *always* apply when you're stuck, i.e., you can't see the wood for the trees? In which case, what might you be able to do to minimize the likelihood of your returning to this spot?

The first four chapters of the book introduce the subject of being stuck, and the different ways of finding solutions to get back on track. They explore more deeply the power of the mind and how we human beings represent challenges internally; the power of metaphor; the lessons nature has to teach us. They also consider common reactions to the process – both positive and negative – so you know what to expect.

Each chapter in Part 2 takes a saying people use when stuck and provides different ways of solving the problem, using the landscape they've used to describe the situation to get back on track.

"I'm stuck in a rut" becomes a conversation about the rut, how they're stuck, how to get unstuck, other places they can now travel within the landscape. We don't get lost in the content of the real situation. We simply explore the patterns that are facilitating the stuckness, and therefore can identify what needs to happen to become unstuck. Perhaps that's why I enjoy using them so much – I love patterns. This may feel weird and you may think you can't do it. You are, however, already doing this every day:

- You have dreams at night that don't make sense but are full of sights and sounds.
- Everyone is an artist and already constructs their own world to make sense of it. You are distorting, generalizing, and deleting information all the time. Distortion is a means of demonstrating your artistry – taking an event and making it your own with a few additions that were never there in the original event. Words that were never spoken, weather events that never occurred and people who weren't even there.
- Artistry is what you're doing every time you pick up a pen, brush, scissors, knife, camera or rolling pin – making sense of the world and depicting it in a way that provides meaning for you.

This process asks that you do the same – it just provides a few rules to allow you to do it.

- Pick a saying that best describes your stuckness.
- Explore the landscape that it conjures up.
- Make changes to that landscape in order to unstuck (changes to what you see, hear, do or feel).

Each chapter is different – it's as if the saying itself has had an impact on the style and format of the chapter that deals with its resolution.

I set out with a format in mind but it turned out that the sayings didn't allow me to do that. Which to me proves the efficacy of the process – if each aspect of stuckness was the same then the solution would always be the same. The differences include:

- Style of questions asked to describe the saying or change it.
- Exploration of the saying.

Trying to make each chapter conform to a specific structure felt as if I was trying to change the essence of the saying. That said, what's been shared is the essence of the saying for me, and those who have used the process with me for nearly 20 years. The essence of the saying for *you* may be the same as described here, or different – so don't be surprised if when reading the chapter on being a fish out of water you suddenly realize you could apply that question to not being able to see the wood for the trees.

You can even take insights from how I've explored one saying and apply it to other sayings. Once you get the knack of the process you'll be able to spread your wings and have some fun with any sayings you're using to describe a situation. I'm just providing examples to give you a sense of those million words we're describing.

Before I go, one last question. What would the benefit be to you of no longer being stuck, of no longer being able to relate to the sayings I'm using?

Spend a little time considering what life could be like if you were no longer facing this problem.

What would you be able to do? How would you feel? What else would you be able to do with your time and other resources?

In other words, provide yourself with the motivation to continue reading. I know it's worth it – I just want you to know that too.

EnJoy.

# PART I

# THE POWER OF THE MIND, METAPHOR AND NATURE

# CHAPTER I

# HELP — I'M STUCK

*There is nothing either good or bad but thinking makes it so.*

William Shakespeare

If we accept the above statement as true, then I'd suggest the same could be said of problems.

If we're stuck, it's because we think we're stuck rather than being a reflection of reality. At a logical level we always know we have choices; there are just times when we can't understand what those choices are, or don't want to take them.

What comes first – the thinking you're stuck or the being stuck? Both can be true:

- You're happily going along and then you become stuck, can't see the wood for the trees and start thinking you're stuck. Solutions escape you.

Or:

- You think you're stuck, you're always stuck, that's just the way you are, muddling through, getting by, but always in a mini state of stuckness.

Either way, it's the belief that you're stuck that will be preventing you from understanding what the solutions are.

There are many different ways of changing a belief – sometimes it's as simple as recognizing it as a belief and not necessarily a true statement of fact, and changing it to something more supportive.

Even "I don't currently know what to do" is more helpful than "I'm stuck".

It's to do with the permanence associated with the word stuck. "I'm stuck" doesn't presuppose anything other than stuckness and continued stuckness. "I'm currently stuck" is a little better because it implies stuckness isn't fixed and can change.

Even the word we're using, therefore, is unhelpful. This is further compounded by the picture we associate with the stuckness.

On the whole, I'm assuming you've picked up this book because you're stuck, and wanting help to get back on track. Or some version of that. It may simply be the stuckness that motivates you to explore an option outlined in the book, or the fact that one or more of the sayings resonate with you.

It's certainly likely that you're unsure what to do in a particular situation. You may already have used one of the sayings listed to describe the current situation you're stuck in, or about. Or you may be so frustrated not knowing what to do about a problem that you'll try anything, and someone suggested this book!

Let's start with the terminology.

**Stuckness** is the term I am using throughout this book.

Words, however, are simply metaphors, and even though I'm saying "stuck" you may describe that stuckness using a number of different words.

To ensure we aren't at cross-purposes – I write "problem" and you think "I don't have a problem, just a hurdle to get over" – see below for examples of terms that you might use for different situations and stages.

| Stuck | How to Get from A to B | Back on Track |
| --- | --- | --- |
| Current situation | Journey | Desired outcome/ situation/state |
| Here and now | Path | Goal/objective |
| Stuck state | Changes | Dream |

| Stuck | How to Get from A to B | Back on Track |
|---|---|---|
| Going round in circles | Reducing barriers | Going with the flow |
| Out on a limb | Find the antidote | Destination |
| Can't see the wood for the trees | Hurdles to get over | On track |
| Stuck in a rut | Options | Feel differently about the same situation |
| Missed the tide | Opportunities | Taking action |
| Like a fish out of water | Alternatives | Moving forward |
| In at the deep end | Different perspectives | Progress |
| Head in the sand | Movement | Shift |
| Current reality | Insight | Transformation |
| Lack of clarity | Remove setbacks | Change |
| Resistant | Release pain | Clarity |
| Problem | Release resistance | Intention |
| Issue | Possibilities | Resolution |
| Challenge | Interpret | Answer |
| Hindered | Remove the interference | Solution |
| Lost | Expand your comfort zone | Outcome |
| Unsure | Unlock potential | Opportunity |
| Blocked | Access inner wisdom | Results |

## Feelings may include:

| Stuck | Back on Track |
|---|---|
| Confused | New way of thinking/ feeling |
| Afraid | Easy |
| Difficult | Effortless |
| Hard work | Free |
| Held back | Motivated |
| Stopped | Inspired |
| Trapped | Empowered |
| Negative | Positive |
| Insecure | Competent |
| Resistant | Liberated |
| Closed | Open |

| Stuck | Back on Track |
| --- | --- |
| Stifled | Connected |
| Bored | Joyful |
| Afraid | Courageous |
| Dissatisfied | Satisfied |
| Unhappy or sad or upset | Happy |
| Lacking confidence | Confident |
| Unresourceful | Resourceful |

Stuck is such a great word to use to describe all these feelings, and yet using this word and others like it without care can contribute to keeping us stuck.

| Stuck | Finding solutions |
| --- | --- |
| Negative | Positive |
| Closed | Open |
| Looking backwards | Looking forwards |
| Nothing will work | Anything might work |
| Same way I've always done it | New ways to do it |
| Fearful of change | Embrace change |
| Scared | Excited |
| Blaming others | Taking personal responsibility |
| Uninspired | Creative & innovative |

See below which emotions being stuck can generate versus the emotions needed to find a solution.

Or perhaps you want to think, not in terms of a "solution", but of an "answer". A client was recently struggling to think of any solutions to a challenge she was facing – until I suggested she look for answers and they came thick and fast! As author and speaker Caroline Myss is very fond of saying, words have power.

I'm not suggesting every one of the above feelings is represented in every situation of stuckness, or when trying to find solutions.

The likelihood, however, is that if you are stuck, a larger percentage of the characteristics on the left will be in play than those on the right, and they'll hinder you finding a solution to get back on track.

There are things we can do to help access the more creative state; these might include changing our environment, listening to music we enjoy, movement, remembering previous times we were very creative, spending time on a creative pastime such as painting, or playing with children, having a bath or reading a good book, and so on.

You may therefore want to think about what has worked best for you in the past to be more resourceful, and do some of that before reading further. You may find a solution to the challenge you're facing simply by doing that.

The techniques described in the book are just other ways to help our mind move from a closed "I don't know what to do" mindset to an open "Oh yes, that's what I could do" mindset.

The challenge is noticing when we're using the landscape to describe a stuck situation, and then understanding what we can do to get back on track.

Each chapter in Part 2 is about you making changes to your life by taking responsibility for yourself, responsibility for what you can do to shift the situation for you.

One underlying presupposition of the book I'd like to highlight here is that we are made up of many different parts. It's the conflict between the differing needs and wants of the many parts, and their differing power over us, that can keep us stuck or set us free.

At its simplest level an example might be the conflict between the part that wants to stay stuck and the part that wants to get back on track. At the moment it may be that the part that wants to stay stuck is shouting the loudest. The process here enables you to turn that stuck part down a little, and to hear better the parts that have access to many different perspectives and potential solutions.

Let's explore this concept a little more. In the morning there may be a part of you that wants to stay in bed when the alarm goes off, and the part that persuades you to get up. Or the part that wants to eat that second piece of chocolate cake and the part, that, while it didn't manage to persuade you not to eat the first piece, does manage to persuade you to walk away from the second piece.

Which results in showing that there is:

- a part of you that loves being stuck;
- a part of you that takes action;

- a part of you that logically knows things;'
- a part of you that intuitively knows things;
- a part of you that feels;
- a part of you that wants more;
- a part of you that's very happy with how life is;
- a part of you that is inspired;
- a part of you that is scared;
- a part of you that wants to change;
- a part of you that doesn't.

The key is aligning all the parts to move in the direction of your goals, and quietening the parts of you that are opposed to taking that action. Or, perhaps putting it better, understanding the concerns of those parts of you so that they quieten themselves.

The techniques in this book will help you listen perhaps a little more intently for advice from these different parts.

If you don't like the idea of being made up of different parts – although of course that's only another metaphor – then simply see these techniques as different or creative ways to access your brain. We all have off days, when we just want a simple life and don't really want to make any decisions, and other days when ideas come to us more easily and effortlessly. These techniques just help the hard-wiring in the brain to bypass the reasons we're stuck and find the location of the solution more easily.

Mixing a few metaphors here, using these techniques is like:

- The telephone number that connects you to the person you want to speak to.
- The map so you can see where you are, the possible destinations and the route options for getting there.

Having discussed the language for the current challenge, and the desired goal, it will now be useful to understand why are we using a metaphor to help shed light on the situation, and why particularly a nature metaphor. The next chapter considers these questions.

# CHAPTER 2

# METAPHORS' AND NATURE'S ABILITY TO HELP YOU FIND SOLUTIONS

When I say "The ball is in your court" or "Can you shed light on the subject?" you know what I mean.

We unconsciously use metaphors in our language all the time, as short cuts to convey meaning to others. Meanings that are richer than just the words themselves. As I said earlier, if a picture paints a thousand words then a metaphor paints a thousand pictures – and so a metaphor provides a million words.

The notion of a million words contained within a metaphor may or may not be completely or scientifically accurate but what I hope it does convey is the richness of metaphors – with their help, we don't have to use thousands upon thousands of words to describe a situation. Which helps when we're trying to solve a problem – surely, after all, the fewer words, and therefore amount of time, we spend talking about it rather than solving it the better?

Have you ever noticed that sometimes the more you talk about a problem the more confused you become? And that the more people are involved, the more barriers and resistance to hearing different ideas there are, and the further away the solution starts to seem?

The challenge when we have any problem is that we can easily get stuck in the content – the detail – and since it's the detail that we're stuck with it's not a surprise that sometimes it's the detail that also KEEPS us stuck.

For example, how easy is it to get caught up in:

- He said this.
- Then she said that.
- And how dare she.
- And then you'll never guess what happened.
- How rude!

and before you know it:

- Unless they apologize I'm never speaking to them again
- I'm just going to do what I wanted to do in the first place – stuff them!
- I'm just going to ignore it.

Or you ask someone to tell you about the problem… and three hours later you're still there as they fill you in with every detail they think you need to hear. All so you can see it the same way as they do!

Other often-used phrases when solution-finding include:

- We've always done it like this.
- If it ain't broke don't fix it.
- We tried that before, and it didn't work then.
- But what will I do then?
- I like doing it this way.
- It won't work.
- We're not going there.
- I don't want to talk about it.
- I'm bored about talking about it.

Or other variants in the same vein that enable us to defend our position and reinforce our own point of view, making it harder and harder to be able to stand back, get some perspective and find a solution.

The problem with trying to solve a challenge using the current logic is, therefore, that we get caught up in that logic and detail. Perhaps more importantly, we strongly hold on to our judgements, beliefs and assessments about the situation, and believe them to be correct. Which means alternatives are not so easy to identify, and consensus is hard to achieve.

Which is where metaphors come in.

Try it for a moment. Let's go with something related to the profession I started out in – purchasing (buying goods and services for organizations). Not the sexiest topic, I know.

What do you think supplier management in organizations involves? Or put another way – once you've placed an order with a supplier, how much thought do you give the supplier? And if you were to give them any thought what do you think their role would involve?

If the many horror stories in the news from my time in procurement are anything to go by – or the conversations I have on flights – then orders are placed and it's just assumed that suppliers will deliver. Until there's a problem, of course!

I find gardening to be a useful metaphor for supplier management; non-purchasing managers (i.e., the bulk of managers in organizations) tend to know more about gardening than about purchasing (that's where the notion of painting a thousand pictures comes in).

Which means that suddenly they start realizing that suppliers need pruning, weeding, mowing, watering, deadheading, composting and maybe even some time in the greenhouse. It opens up a whole new conversation about:

- How many suppliers are like that tree whose roots are undermining the foundations of the house?
- What to do with weed-like suppliers who pop up everywhere?
- Who is in charge of the tool shed, and keeping the tools sharpened?
- Who's the gardener and who do they report to?
- What's the objective for the garden?
- What soil do you have?
- What type of plants thrive in this environment?
- How many plants do you want?
- Do you want all-year-round colour, or just summer colour?
- Will you have a compost heap, and if so when to spread it about?

Can you get a sense that saying "Purchasing is like gardening" has opened and speeded up the conversation in a way that talking about purchasing theory might not have done?

It's not just gardening; many nature metaphors can be used to better effect than talking about any subject we know more about than the other person!

For example, we might decide the solution to a problem is to be more bear- or eagle-like; those few words can convey so much more...

- Bear – courageous, strong, nurturing, tenacious, resilient
- Eagle – attentive, visionary, adventurous, confident

Or when looking at a tree we might notice:

- The roots – and consider how we can keep grounded in our own life.
- The branches – and acknowledge how we too can be as flexible and yet as strong as possible in our own actions.
- The leaves – and realize that for many trees, these grow new each year in the spring and are dropped in the autumn, reminding us of the ebb and flow of nature – nothing fixed, just evolving and growing.
- The wood – reminding us of the need to collaborate and work with others.
- The path through the wood – pointing us in the direction of developing a plan to help us achieve our goal.

Metaphors are, however, in the eye of the beholder. That is, our minds are meaning-making machines, and are very good at noticing the pattern within a metaphor that applies to us and our situation, and ignoring everything else within the metaphor that doesn't.

You may therefore have got different insights from the tree example than those listed above. Thankfully that's not a problem, because it's your interpretation that will provide insight for you, and mine that will provide insight for me. For example, using the bear and eagle as a metaphor could have brought to mind for you the vicious aspects of their nature and not those I've listed. For your life, at this time, it just means that is the insight you need, and not the one I observed and obviously needed.

There is no right or wrong with metaphors – all they do is open up a conversation so that the current situation, barriers to change, options, opportunities and the desired outcome are seen from a different perspective. This enables solutions to be found regarding what action to take, and allows progress to be made.

For example, a TV programme I watched recently explained how frogspawn will not develop if there are insufficient resources in the pond to allow the tadpoles to thrive. Instead the spawn hangs back until the conditions are right.

As you read this information what insight can you take from it as it relates to your life, and even about why you're reading this book today?

For me, as I write this chapter, it's about recognizing that conditions might not be perfect; they might not be what I'd wished for – but as the presenter said "Who wants to be a tadpole for ever?" This metaphor might therefore inspire me to take action – today.

Someone else reading it, who might be wondering if they're procrastinating, might take from it that it's OK to wait until the conditions are right.

No right or wrong, just different perspectives from which to view the situation we want insight on.

The beauty of using metaphor to explore problem resolution, especially if you can stick with the metaphor for as long as possible, is that it avoids:

- ego
- resistance
- barriers
- "ifs", "buts", "nots" and "can'ts"
- defensiveness
- anger
- blame

The beauty of using metaphor to explore opportunities is it avoids all of the above, and in addition avoids:

- attachment to preconceived opportunities;
- the same old opportunities re-emerging time and time again;
- lack of new ideas emerging.

With metaphors from nature the suggestion to try something different can come from:

- walking along a lane and seeing a hole in the hedge towards pastures new;
- sunrise or sunset, reminding us of the constant beginnings and, endings in life;
- caterpillars or butterflies, pointing us towards transformation processes;
- seeds – whether floating past, growing or still in their pods/shells – helping us tap into our own inner seed bank of creativity;
- the tide changing, showing us that nothing ever stays the same;
- harvest time, acknowledging that the hard work has to be done first;
- springtime, a reminder of new beginnings.

I can assure you that the "can'ts" evaporate when faced with the wisdom of nature. Once the wisdom has been harvested, then, and only then, is it time to release the metaphor. Time to understand what it means in practice and to identify an inspirational and innovative strategy for you going forward.

## Nature

We use nature all the time in the language we use – stuck in a rut, out on a limb, and so on.

The premise is that if we're using the saying then at some level, in our mind the saying, and the landscape contained with it, represent the current situation. If we're currently stuck, therefore, one way to get unstuck is to change the image representing it. Why nature specifically, though, and not just any metaphor we use in our rich language?

Many have written about the ability of nature to provide perspective on our lives:

*"Look deep into nature and you will understand everything better."*

Albert Einstein

*"In every walk with nature one receives far more than he seeks."*

John Muir

*"It is the marriage of the soul with nature that makes the intellect fruitful, and gives birth to imagination."*

Henry David Thoreau

Why does nature have such a hold on us? For me there are many different aspects to the answer.

For supplier management, in my role as a buyer, I found that using the gardening metaphors discussed above was much better for helping managers than just talking about how to manage their suppliers better.

It worked so well that I expanded the model to use landscapes as metaphors for our lives, and the rest is history. Over the years in my coaching and facilitation work with organizations and individuals, I've led many hundreds of sessions involving walking around outside in nature developing strategies and solving problems.

When describing problems we're not restricted to nature metaphors. For example no pain no gain, outside of my comfort zone, juggling balls or spinning plates are all metaphors that could be explored in order to find a solution. However, nature is something we can all relate to – it's everywhere in our language (as we have seen already) and we all know something about it – we see it every day and it impacts our every waking moment, even if only through the air we breathe.

Nature produces the base materials for everything we use every day of our lives. Perhaps the closer to nature we are the more we are able to be ourselves, untainted by a world constantly trying to alter or enhance something that is already beautiful. Is it a coincidence that those trapped in the offices in the very centres of our cities are the same financiers who lost their sense of what it was to be authentic, to have integrity and respect, and whose greed led to the crash of 2008?

Perhaps the reason we "make mountains out of molehills" is because we need mountains in our lives. There's something very fulfilling about getting to the top of a mountain – especially if it's higher than all the surrounding mountains. We achieve that milestone at the end of a struggle, along with a sense of achievement, and knowing it's going to be much easier from here on in. Although anyone with bad knees will tell you that going downhill is worse (ouch).

What nature teaches, which is very valuable for us, is that it's useful to understand the natural order of things – for example to understand how to read the clouds (people) and atmosphere (culture); to forecast the weather (behaviours); or to understand how seeds (ideas) grow – otherwise we end up planting the seed in winter, and wondering why it failed to flourish.

Don't we do that often in life – just rush headlong into new projects, and forget to place that project into a context of the natural order of things?

I wonder – do we use these sayings also because we crave a connection with nature?

Would someone who is often in nature use these sayings more, or less, than someone who rarely leaves the city or suburbia?

I don't know the answer, but I do think a connection with nature is ingrained into our DNA, with an energetic connection underlying every breath we take. Nature has produced or cleansed the oxygen to allow us to breathe, nature provides the water we drink and nature produces the food we eat. Perhaps produces is the wrong word – provides the nutrients to allow the food to flourish. Anyway, we undoubtedly flourish because nature does.

Nature is something we can all relate to, albeit in different ways; we all have different feelings about different locations or landscapes. Here's a blog I wrote some time ago that might help explain what I mean.

I went to the top of Glastonbury Tor at the weekend and it was beautifully sunny, if also very cold and windy. Once at the top I managed to get right up against the Tor and shelter from the wind and spent over an hour and half there.

A tweet I sent while there reflected that it's one of the few places in the world where I am able to stop. I don't fidget. I don't feel the need to move. I don't feel the need to do much. I wouldn't say lots of thinking goes on either. Generally, I just look out, and chat with others who join me for their 15 minutes at the top.

On further reflection I realize that this is a place that helps me be more grounded – a trait I can sometimes misplace, which then allows the headless chicken to take control.

I wondered about the different places that I visit – each helps me achieve a different state:

- Glastonbury, England – Grounding
- Findhorn, Scotland – Intuiting
- Keswick, the Lake District, England – Peaceful
- Bamburgh, Northumberland, England – Relaxed
- Florida – Laughing
- Sydney/New York – Inspired
- Uluru, Australia – Connected

I think my current home here in Burntisland, Scotland perhaps offers a little of all of these, which is why I stay even though so much of my work is down south or further afield.

We often think our state is determined by what's happening to us – a bad day means a bad mood, a good day the opposite, a long-awaited meeting possibly apprehension, our first date excitement. It's true these events can lead to us choosing to feel that way. We do, however, have a choice. It's not the bad day that directly led to a bad mood – in between there was a choice made about our response to the day.

In situations where we're finding it hard to get into a resourceful state of mind and body our imagination can help us achieve the desired state. I might not be able to go to Sydney every time I want to be inspired but I can tap into the people, books, films, clothes, colours and music of Sydney that help me become inspired.

What state would help you most today and what could you to do to access it more easily?

Like me, can you think of different landscapes that generate different feelings and thoughts for you?

Even an imaginary landscape can do the same. As I imagine standing on the top of any of the world's great mountains and looking at the view, I can't help but take a deep breath and relax. Is it just me, or do you do that too? It seems to me to be a reflex associated with that landscape.

It is not too much of a leap from this association with landscapes, therefore, to suggest that we can choose a landscape to represent our current situation, and a landscape that depicts the antidote – where we're headed.

What the Landscaping Your Life process is inviting us to do is choose a landscape we associate with a situation, and then analyze it. It's as if by getting the landscape out in front of us we can see what we're missing. We allow the metaphor (the landscape) to represent our problem so that we can make sense of it more fully and ultimately, therefore, find solutions.

We can see patterns everywhere we look in nature, whether in:

plants

water

weather patterns

We often forget that there are also patterns in our own behaviour, some supportive and others less so. Patterns that support you achieving your goals, and/or patterns that set you back.

- Patterns may be fairly clear to see: watching TV, or using the laptop until after midnight every night and then struggling to get up in the morning, and not having as much energy as you'd like throughout the day.
- Patterns may be hidden: the tone and words used by the small voice within that repeatedly talks us out of action.
- Patterns may be totally unconscious: only really observable over time when we eventually realize we ALWAYS give up too soon, back off from conflict, eat too much when stressed, play it safe, avoid the unknown, and so on.

No pattern is inherently good or bad. The clue is in the outcome that it delivers. If it's not an outcome that you want, and you can understand the pattern that triggers the response, you simply have to change the pattern. (OK, that is perhaps not always "simple", but understanding the unresourceful pattern is a major step towards success.) The beauty of using nature to interpret our patterns is that people don't get defensive about how many trees are in the wood, and which ones need to be chopped down. Whereas you might get very defensive if I jumped straight in and asked how much time you spent on social media, and how you were going to reduce it. By the time you've decided you need to metaphorically cut some trees down, you're likely to be much more open to then looking at what that means in reality, and realizing that time on Twitter can be reduced.

As you explore the sayings in each chapter I'm sure you'll find out for yourself how rich nature is, and how easy is it to find parallels between nature and our lives. A flourishing landscape provides for a flourishing life.

There might, however, also be a deeper reason why nature works so well – one that's perhaps more spiritual in its origins. Many people have written about a human need for connection with nature – as the quotes from John Muir, Einstein and Henry David Thoreau at the start of the chapter demonstrate.

We came from the stars – not in a spaceship sort of way but as part of the Big Bang that resulted in the development of the stars and planets. We are made up of the same stuff as nature – we are nature.

It's what all existing indigenous cultures know and what our forefathers knew. We're inextricably linked to nature; therefore why wouldn't the solutions to our problems lie in nature?

Nature is the one true constant. It is solid ground, fluid water, energy-giving air that has been there for millennia, providing support for all that have asked for it. The sun follows the night, high tide follows low tide, ocean follows river that in turn follows stream.

In this book you're being invited by nature to remember what's often forgotten in this busy world, and to look into nature's silence to provide the answers you're craving. Peace for the busy, direction for the lost, beauty for the angry, calm for the fearful and connection for the lonely. And to trust your representation of it, and trust that by following nature's ways, you can find the solution – to shift from stuck to flow, from closed to open, from not knowing to knowing.

The next chapter explains more about how the Landscaping Your Life process works.

# CHAPTER 3

# HOW THE LANDSCAPING YOUR LIFE PROCESS WORKS

The premise of this book is that the metaphorical landscape contained within your language can be used to unlock the challenge you're describing and help you get back on track. For example, if you feel that you can't see the wood for the trees, it may be that the trees have some light to shed – leading, potentially, to the solution. Perhaps you need to stop focusing on the individual trees, or need to cut some of the trees back; which might translate into needing to focus on your goal and not get lost in the detail, or needing to manage your time better by not doing everything yourself.

The aim is to guide you from your current situation to a desired outcome. If you're happy with the current situation, there's no reason to look for an alternate outcome because you're already there. If you're less than happy (dissatisfied, lacking in confidence, fearful, unsure, bored, confused), looking for alternatives might be helpful.

The current stuck situation and the desired back on track outcome can be expressed in many different ways through many different terms, as can the means of moving from one to the other. You may therefore want to return to the list of words in Chapter 1 that I use throughout the book and that have also been used by clients who were stuck, and who have experienced the transformative impact of the process. Which means, if any of the terms listed resonate with you, that you can be assured that someone in a similar situation used the Landscaping Your Life (LYL from now on) process and obtained insight as a result.

The main underlying theory of the LYL process is the use of landscapes as metaphors for a situation, where solutions are found within the metaphorical landscape. The aim when using the process is to therefore keep the current real-life situation at the back of your mind, and not allow the "this means that" to creep back in, until the process is finished. In other words, to find out, via the metaphor, what the solution might be. You don't therefore have to understand initially why the situation is like a wood, and what the trees represent. The aim is to use what you know about trees and woods to help you find a solution – for example, you may just need to be more grounded like the roots of the trees, or more flexible like the branches.

This chapter provides you with a broader explanation of the processes used in each chapter – which means you can expand any exploration of a landscape in any of the chapters, and adapt it to account for your own unique metaphorical landscape and preferences.

The process to follow for each of the chapters is as follows:

1. **Anchor a positive landscape – feel safe, secure, happy.**
2. **Determine the current situation you'd like some insight on.**
3. **Pick a saying that best describes the current situation.**
4. **Put the real-life situation to the back of your mind.**
5. **Explore the metaphorical landscape.** – Options include:
   - Identify an action plan as if you were really in the landscape described by the saying – how could you see the wood for the trees?
   - Describe the current landscape using the sayings as a prompt.
   - Describe the current landscape without using the sayings.
   - Explore it some more – use pictures, maps, collage.
   - Explore a real landscape.
   - Make changes to the current landscape, and allow it to become the desired landscape.
   - Go on an imagined journey from the current landscape to the desired landscape.
   - Stand in the shoes of someone who can see the wood for the trees, i.e., is out of a rut.
6. **Revisit the original real-life situation – and notice what you notice.**

Here's more about what each step involves:

## 1. Anchor a positive landscape – feel safe, secure, happy

Since we're using metaphors, it's not that likely you'll end up feeling worse than when you started. However, it would be remiss of me not to acknowledge the possibility. For example, I might ask you to consider standing somewhere or next to something that, unbeknown to me, makes you feel frightened due to a phobia or past experience.

For the (likely) very rare occasions, therefore, where you're feeling out of sorts and uncomfortable with where the process has taken you and, more importantly, with where you still are, it's useful to know you have something up your sleeve that you can use to get you back into a more resourceful state of mind and body.

It's called an anchor, and it's called that because it's something you can use to bring you back to a positive and resourceful feeling. To do that:

- Think about a landscape you really like – one that makes you feel positive, confident, happy and/or secure (or any other feeling that you associate with feeling resourceful and satisfied). You can use a picture of the landscape, or just imagine the landscape itself or a memory of being in it. Take some time to choose the right landscape – there's no rush.
- Once you've picked the landscape/memory, give it a name.
- Fully concentrate on imagining the landscape/memory – the colours, textures, sounds, sights, feelings, weather and so on. Really bring the landscape alive. Say its name out loud – or if in public, in your mind. Keep concentrating on the image for perhaps ten seconds, while the feeling is still very positive. If you feel yourself getting distracted, or losing the peak positive feeling, stop imagining the landscape.
- Think of something else for a moment – something that brings about a different feeling; perhaps what you're going to do later, or what's for lunch. Anything that breaks your state.
- Bring to mind the landscape again, and say its name out loud, imagining it for a further ten seconds or so. Stop just before the good feeling starts to reduce.

> • Repeat steps 4–5 until, as soon as you think of the word or say it out loud, you feel confident, positive and happy.

You now have the ability to access that positive feeling at any point – whether when reading this book, or in life more generally. All you have to do is say or think the word you used to anchor that feeling, and the feeling will follow.

This anchor is now available to you should any question I ask, or landscape you take yourself into, take you into a state you do not wish to be in. Of course, discomfort isn't necessarily always to be avoided, but this process isn't about taking you from a stuck state and leaving you in an even more stuck state. Your anchor image will allow you to get back to where you started easily and effortlessly whenever you feel the need for returning there.

Let's now consider the situation you'd like more clarity about.

## 2. Determine the current situation you'd like some insight on

Before reading any of the chapters it's useful to consider a situation where you could use, or are already using, the saying to describe it. For example:

> • Whether to accept a job
> • Whether to move house
> • How to resolve a problem with a family member
> • How to communicate with a colleague
> • What direction to take your career in next
> • How to handle bullying behaviour at work or home
> • How to prioritize your to-do list
> • Feeling more confident
> • Releasing what's holding you back
> • Getting healthier or fitter
> • Becoming more financially secure

Pick a situation that you feel stuck about, that you're fighting against the flow, that is hard work, and wouldn't it be great if it was much easier, or you had more clarity about what to do.

It doesn't have to be a big problem, just a challenge that you'd like some additional insight on.

Next consider your answer to the following questions:

- How satisfied do you feel about the situation on a scale of 0–10?
- What benefit would it provide if you felt more satisfied?
- How long have you been stuck?

The reason I ask this last question is that your answer will determine my recommendation about what to do next.

If you're generally on track about all areas of your life, and this is a specific blip about a specific area of your life such as what to do about a problem at work, or how to deal with a relationship, then do just pick the saying that best describes how you're feeling about the situation and go straight to that chapter.

If you've been stuck for some time, and that stuckness has perhaps spread out into a number of areas in your life, I'd recommend reading all the chapters about all the sayings in sequence. Resolving being stuck in a rut would then help provide the motivation, and seeing the wood for the trees would then help identify the outcome thereafter, and so on. This is important if you've been stuck for some time and gets you moving again.

The questions I ask in each chapter are not exhaustive – yes, I've tested and used them with others for years, but every time I work with someone one-to-one I ask subtly different questions.

Each of our landscapes is unique; I just ask questions that I hope will inspire a train of thought, to get you moving again.

You could therefore spend some time away from the book exploring your metaphorical landscape so you can see what changes need to be made to the current landscape to make it better. Use the questions outlined in Part 3 to help you do this.

## 3. Pick a saying that best describes the current situation

With your current stuck situation in mind, consider which of the following sayings used in the book best describes the situation.

- Making mountains out of molehills
- Stuck in a rut
- Can't see the wood for the trees
- Up the creek without a paddle
- Like a fish out of water
- Head in the sand
- Out on a limb/In at the deep end
- Treading water/Going round in circles
- Missed the tide

Don't worry that it may feel odd, nor wonder if it makes sense. Just trust that a part of you does know, and it's that part you're going to take on a journey around the landscape to help find a solution.

## 4. Put the real-life situation to the back of your mind

Once you've chosen the saying that describes your current situation you need to put the real-life situation to the back of your mind. If at all possible identify the situation, score it and then put it in an imaginary "box" to open again later, i.e., don't keep opening the box to check how the metaphor might apply. It's like trying to watch a seed grow – you can't dig it up every five minutes.

It's very important that you stay in the metaphor for as long as possible, and only think about the actual situation once you've fully explored the metaphor/landscape.

This is the one instruction for which I wish I could be by your side while you're trying it out, to ensure that you follow it!

Your mind WILL want to switch back to real life as soon as it can. You may find yourself saying "What does this mean in reality" or "What does the creek or paddle mean or represent?" Doing this too soon is just like trying to solve the problem logically, and all the reasons you haven't resolved it thus far will stop you from finding a solution this time too.

I recently took six suit-wearing business executives for a walk into some local woods. They took it in turn to describe the current situation, and to choose a saying that best described their stuckness. There's a lot of power in saying, for example, that you "can't see the wood for the trees" while in a real-life wood, because the wood can provide solutions. However, they repeatedly tried to link the wood to the current situation. By doing that they were losing such a large percentage of the metaphor. I may not know why the tree I've chosen relates more to the situation than another tree, or why that direction is better than another. Spending time trying to relate the direction in the wood to a direction in real life diminishes the effectiveness of the process.

One reason it's to be avoided is that we're revisiting the stuckness state, and so often the conversation gets back round to justifying why we're stuck – "I've tried that", "it won't work", "I don't know what to do." The aim has to be to stay away from the current situation for as long as possible. Assess how it feels not to be able to see the wood for the trees, and use that assessment within the landscape to determine what your next action should be.

Here's one example of how easy it is for us to get distracted away from the metaphor and a potential solution, and back to real life.

Jan was exploring not being able to see the wood for the trees. She then saw a logjam in a river and said that was what it was like: "I'm stuck one side of the logjam, and want to get to the other side."

As we looked at the logjam we discussed different ways of getting rid of it – pushing it away (although we did wonder if the logs might then float down the river, and cause another one in the future), climbing over them, allowing a beaver to use them elsewhere in the river, imagining them as balloon logs that we could pop.

Before she could envisage doing any of these to her representation, however, she said "I'll perhaps feel more able to do this when I get back from my holidays." In other words, she brought real life back into the assessment – and was finding a diversion to avoid releasing the block.

When we're using metaphors, things that are happening to us in real life don't apply in the same way. In this instance, we needed to explore the saying that best described the desire to put it on hold – perhaps it was burying her head in the sand, or missing the tide. We also needed to explore why she was so quick to decide the problem was no longer about not seeing the wood for the trees – this may or may not have been related to the head-in-the-sand aspect.

If I could remind you of this on every page, I would do so. It is the most important part of the process.

Another reason why reading ALL the sayings in the book is helpful is because they take you on a journey to explore all the potential barriers to success.

Each chapter identifies the options available to explore the saying you've chosen, each one focusing more on one or two of the options than the others. This is just because they made most sense to me in relation to that saying. Other options may make more sense to you, that is quite individual.

Here's a summary to give you a sense of the possibilities.

## 5. Explore the metaphorical landscape

So far, you've set up a positive anchor, identified a situation you'd like more insight on, assessed the level of satisfaction with it, picked a saying/landscape that best describes the situation and put the real-life situation to the back of your mind.

Now time to play! It's time to explore the landscape to uncover what insight it has to share.

- Identify an action plan as if you were really in the landscape described by the saying – how could you see the wood for the trees?
- Describe the current landscape, using the sayings as a prompt.
- Describe the current landscape without using the sayings.
- Explore it some more. Use pictures, maps, collage.
- Explore a real landscape.
- Make changes to the current landscape and allow it to become the desired landscape.
- Go on an imagined journey from the current landscape to the desired landscape.
- Stand in the shoes of someone who can see the wood for the trees, and who is well and truly out of a rut, etc.

Here's more about each of these.

### Identify an action plan as if you were really in the landscape described by the saying

If for example, you were up the creek without a paddle, what would you do? How would you get out of the creek? The chapter on this metaphor provides a great example of exploring the situation using this option.

The aim is to come up with an action plan of how to get out of a rut if you were in one in reality, or to be able to see the wood for the trees, or stop going round in circles.

It may seem a very simplistic question, but remember you're using the saying to describe the situation – your unconscious somehow knows how it relates, and exploring the saying will provide guidance on the plan to move forward.

If you can't imagine that, then imagine instead what a role model of yours would do in the situation?

As the sayings are nature-based, you may want to think about what someone who is very comfortable in that landscape would do – what about Ray Mears or David Attenborough or Ben Fogle? They'd all be great in the woods, or up a creek! They might have knowledge about how to get a boat moving forward when you've lost your paddle, or understand how to use the flow of the river to guide you to the shore, or know how to attract attention from others on the shore.

The aim is to access different parts of you to find a solution (and each of the questions in the relevant chapter allows you to do that in a different way).

Remember, some part of you will let you know what's the appropriate action to take; an action that enables you to move from being stuck to moving forward and being back on track.

The answer may however lie in exploring the landscape more fully.

### Describe the current landscape, using the sayings as a prompt

That's all there is to it really – describe the imaginary and constructed landscape. What are you imagining seeing, hearing, feeling, smelling and even tasting? It's as if you're describing the landscape to someone so they can paint it – or doing the voiceover for a TV programme: "On the right of the scene is a large tree with large roots spreading in every direction…"

The individual chapters in Part 2 and Part 3 provide prompts about what you might want to pay attention to. They allow you to explore the different characteristics that any landscape might have.

If at any point you're not understanding the questions I'm asking, you might want to consider whether it's because our interpretation of the saying, and therefore the landscape, is different. I will try to share my interpretation – if, however, your interpretation is different from mine, please do use the rest of this chapter, and the questions provided in Chapter 16, for more advice to help yourself interpret your metaphorical landscape.

You may find that just describing the landscape is enough for you to feel as if you're already back on track – that now you've got more perspective on the situation you know what you need to do. Perhaps the rut you thought you were in isn't really a rut, and it's easy to know what to do now you're now longer imagining it as a rut.

### Describe the current landscape without using the sayings

Instead of picking a saying, you could just pick a landscape that best depicts the current situation, and then follow the options outlined in this chapter to explore the landscape. This is how I use the process with clients. The sayings just provide an easier means of giving guid-ance when I can't be there to coach you.

If you'd like to try this approach, I'd suggest reading the 'Can't see the wood for the trees' chapter to give you a sense of what's possible.

Once you feel comfortable with the process then any of the options in this chapter can be applied to your landscape. Remember the aim is to change the landscape to enable movement to take place.

### Explore it some more – Use pictures, maps, collage

Thus far, I've assumed we're just verbally exploring the landscape. You might however want to draw it (yes, with coloured pens and paper), or outline a map of how it all fits together, or even get your scissors and glue out and make a collage to depict it. When doing any of these you may find that the creative act of, for example, making the collage provides a clue as to the direction in which the solution will be found.

### Explore a real landscape

At other times, going into nature and making the journey can be helpful – whether that be walking deep in the woods or visiting fields or the ocean. Yes –really physically stepping out of that rut.

To do this you should identify the situation requiring insight, pick a saying and then go for a walk. It might be preferable, certainly the first time you use this process, to choose a landscape described by the saying. It's not essential though, as you'll discover when you try it, and as you read the later chapters.

If you go alone you may want to think about something completely different as you walk, and then tell yourself the story of your walk at the end, and notice what insight you may get.

Alternatively, you may want to consciously look for clues as you walk – noticing the hidden pathway, the light and shadow, the stream, clouds or whatever else makes sense to you.

If you're with another person, it can be very helpful to act out the saying in the landscape – for example if you're "going round in circles" do exactly that, and discuss how you're feeling and even try to walk in one direction. What's stopping you from making a choice as to which direction to go in? Is it really a circle? How do you feel as you walk round in circles?

On one such walk my clients and I observed numerous flies swarming around a cowpat!! A great reminder that not all insights are going to be profound – but this observation did remind us that just because everyone is doing it, doesn't mean it's what we want to be doing.

### Make changes to the current landscape and allow it to become the desired landscape

The assumption is that the current image represents the stuck state. To get unstuck requires making changes to the original image.

We each give different characteristics to our imagined landscapes, and these characteristics have more or less impact on situations and our level of stuckness, e.g., changing colour may make a huge difference – positive or negative. So while I may find meaning in describing something as getting more colourful, it may have more meaning for you if it gets less colourful.

That said, when playing around with these characteristics you may well discount something early on only to find that it has meaning later.

For example, I asked a client, Cheryl, who was "treading water", if changing the light in her imagination made a difference, and she said making it lighter made it scarier. We left the light level as it was for the time being. However, once the water had become warmer and her feet were on the ground then it became lighter of its own accord.

The aim therefore is to find the changes that make the constructed landscape look, sound or feel better, and that may even change other characteristics of the landscape for the better too.

The process is:

- Envisage the landscape that depicts the current situation we're feeling stuck about.
- Decide what changes need to be made to the current landscape to make it just right, and imagine making those changes (warmer, colder, more colour, more greenery, more or less cloud or sun, louder or softer sounds, etc. See the individual chapters in Parts 2 and 3 for more of an idea of what might be changed).
- Make the changes outlined.
- Then, and only once the above steps have been completed, consider what action is required to achieve your desired outcome in reality. It's important that up until now you've stayed in the metaphor, and only think about the actual situation once you've fully explored the metaphor/landscape.
- It may sound a little – or a lot! – weird, but your mind will be able to make sense of it, enabling links to be set up in your brain to bridge the gap between where you are and what needs to happen to get where you want to be.

Basically, your mind is able to make the connection, and will do all the hard work for you.

Relax and continue to explore the image, knowing that as you do so different connections in your brain are being made that will enable you to view the original situation differently.

### *Go on an imagined journey from the current landscape to the desired landscape.*

Of course, the current landscape may never be the solution. It may be the problem; and finding a solution may require movement away from where you are into a new landscape.

There's a number of ways this can be achieved:

1. Envisage a landscape that depicts the current situation we're feeling stuck about.
2. Envisage a landscape that depicts the desired outcome (there is no right or wrong, just what landscape comes to mind immediately or intuitively).
3. Plot a course from one landscape to the other, and then think about what you would need to do to get from one to the other.
4. Then, and only once steps 1–3 have been completed, consider what action is required to achieve your desired outcome in reality. It's important you stay in the metaphor for as long as possible, and only think about the actual situation once you've explored the metaphor/landscape.

Other options include:

- Imagining moving around the landscape. To do this you can either view the landscape from a different perspective, or move to a more agreeable part of the landscape.

I remember once a situation that had me in a desert – no amount of imagining could make that desert any less hot or more pleasant, despite the fact that I knew what my end goal was. This can happen from time to time and will be impacted by the situation you're dealing with.

I could certainly describe the current situation as a landscape, and I could describe the desired state as a landscape too, but every time I tried to change the current landscape into the desired state it kept switching back. I needed to do something to anchor the desired state to enable that to be a realistic option rather than simply a desire. The part of me that had been resisting for some time continued to do so because it hadn't been presented with an acceptable route or means of moving from the current to the desired state.

Let's think about this non-metaphorically for a moment. If I'm currently in Edinburgh, and I want to go to London, I have to travel to get there. Sometimes it's enough to call someone on videophone, and to see London via the screen, but at other times you actually need to go on the physical journey from A to B.

That's what I did when I was in the desert – I imagined walking, and as I did so I started to see trees and bushes; and it became less hot. As I kept walking, slowly the desert became the desired land-scape. A landscape I could anchor and imagine myself being in, because I'd slowly got there, not clicked my fingers and materialized there.

A castaway's choice of track on *Desert Island Discs* once described life as being like a river: water coming from high in the mountain, then joining streams and eventually becoming the river. A great reminder that the solution to your situation might be through music. If you're musically minded, how might the journey from your current situation to your desired outcome sound? If you can, why not write the score, hum the soundtrack or sing the lyrics? Or simply sit or stand at your favourite instrument, and notice what happens as you ad lib the journey in sound.

Those of you not so musically minded might want to dance the journey, or develop a set of movements or gestures that express how it might look and feel to leave the current situation and head for your goal.

I'd still suggest these would all be better if you kept them as representing the metaphor, rather than real life, although later you could try doing that too.

I'd always thought that the ideal route from A to B would be easily agreed upon. Until I realized that my friend and I always go a different route to get to places. I had thought it was because she knew the area better than me, until I realized that, even once she'd shown me her best route, I still didn't take it. I don't know what criteria she uses but I assume she chooses the shortest route. I like to keep moving, so I am prepared for the length of my journey to be a little longer, if it means not being stopped at traffic lights or junctions. I think we both believe our routes to be the best – she thinks the shortest route will deliver that, and I think not having to stop will deliver that.

When considering moving about your metaphorical landscape, therefore, you may want to understand your normal preference for which route to take, and what might be most desirable in this situation. Options might include minimizing stops, finding the quickest or shortest route as the crow flies and/or or cost. If you apply each of these in turn to your landscape (remembering not to fall back into reality and keeping it firmly in that box), what do you notice?

There will be times when moving within your landscape that you're not sure which direction to go in. That's something you'll read more about in the going with the flow chapter.

The going with the flow chapter will help you to keep on track, to avoid the ruts and woods and feeling out of water. The solution, as you will find when you get there, is about heading for the ocean. Whenever you're using a saying, therefore, and you're not sure what to do, you may want to ask yourself:

Am I headed for the ocean?

Don't worry if it makes no sense – Colin, one of the suit-wearing executives from the wood in the story I shared earlier, was able to easily say which direction would take him to the ocean despite us being nowhere near it and not knowing in reality which direction the ocean was. However, the part of him that knew what the ocean meant for him knew what he needed to do, and what he needed to stop doing, and in which direction the ocean was.

I'd suggest that in any journey where you get bogged down with "This direction or that direction?", you have a quick read of the going with the flow chapter.

*Stand in the shoes of someone who can see the wood for the trees, and who is well and truly out of a rut, etc.*

If you're still not getting much insight thus far you may wish to imagine exploring the landscape as another person – here's some suggestions for when you're up the creek without a paddle:

**A character from a book?** I remember on a training session asking my clients what Harry Hole, the detective from Jo Nesbo's crime novels, would do and they said "Go to the pub on his own and sit in a corner." This advice perhaps doesn't particularly relate to the metaphor of the saying, but for some that might be all you need to do!

**Your child?** Children are such great teachers – emotions felt in the moment, and then on to the next emotion, problems soon forgotten and judgements and grudges never held on to. Having watched children playing in the trees in Prince's Gardens in Edinburgh recently, I'd suggest that if they were up the creek without a paddle, they wouldn't care. They'd just find ways to explore the boat or water, play hide-and-seek and just wait for someone to save them.

**And older or younger you.** They may see it as an exciting adventure to see where they ended up, or as having time to explore the creek more. They may be less stressed by the situation, and trust that a solution will be found. Stress can certainly stop us accessing those parts that have the solution. It's as if the answers don't come out until the weather conditions are just right; stress can be like a storm keeping the solutions hidden somewhere, even if they are in a shelter being kept safe and dry. A metaphor in its own right that could provide insight about how to coax the solutions out of the shelter, whether by imagining reducing the wind, the sun shining or putting warmer clothes on in order to weather the storm.

What all these processes are doing is trying to nudge our mind out of its current way of thinking.

## 6. Revisit the original real-life situation

Once you've fully explored the situation metaphorically, using the landscape and nature, it's important to return to the original situation and observe what you notice about it now.

Consider what actions may come to mind, who needs to know about them and when you will take them. You may find that you go through a few stages to get back on track – the end result may be laughter, an ah-ha moment, a shift in stance or simply a recognition that something has changed and you have clarity about what you want to do.

You may not know what to do – you may just feel different and, on your satisfaction scale of 0–10, realize you're at a higher level than when you started.

Sometimes the release has taken place unconsciously, and it's the feelings that have changed – you don't have to "know" what's changed or what you need to do differently. That will just happen now the barriers have been removed.

At other times you may need to logically consider what cutting a few trees down might look like in reality. What is that insight asking you to do – what do you need to reduce the number of?

On your scale of 0–10 how satisfied do you feel about the situation? What action have you decided to take, who needs to know about it and when will you take it?

**Checklist before starting each chapter**

Remember the premise of this book:

- The saying represents a current situation that, for want of a better word, you're stuck about.
- Your goal is to get on track, and move towards a new desired outcome.
- The saying uses a landscape so the landscape is taken to represent the current situation.
- The aim therefore is to make changes to the landscape until it represents a non-stuck state.
- This non-stuck state may either take you towards your desired outcome, or represent it.

The key thing to remember is not every suggestion in the book will work for every group or person or every situation, and not everyone will be comfortable with all of the ideas. It's about finding a tool you *are* comfortable with.

If you're stuck and would like to explore the potential solutions from a different perspective, the process to follow is:

- Pick a situation you'd like some clarity on – determine how satisfied you feel about it on a scale of 0–10.
- Identify which of the sayings best describes the current situation.
- Read the chapter on that saying (and make changes to the current landscape.)
- Assess your level of satisfaction about the situation (0–10).
- If satisfaction is higher than when you started, decide if you're OK to leave it there or want to see if you can increase it further.

You may find as you make changes or end up in a new landscape that it has aspects of another of the sayings. For example, as the river meets the sea you may start to feel you might have missed the tide – so pop along to that chapter just to get a sense of whether you may need to explore that constructed landscape too.

While I've provided in each chapter my interpretation of the solution to be found in each saying, that doesn't mean there aren't other interpretations. Remember, the premise throughout the book is that you already have the solution – you're just not yet listening to the part of you that knows. Before reading any chapter, therefore, especially where the saying being used really resonates with you, you may wish to spend a little time exploring the saying first to see if you can start a dialogue with the part of you that knows.

If at any time throughout the chapter you find that a specific word jars or feels out of sync, it just means I've made an assumption that the landscape includes that component. For example, I may write "river" but your landscape may include a stream, a road, a valley or something else – I just chose the most likely component from my perspective for the purposes of the examples used.

Don't ever feel the need to add a component I've mentioned into your landscape; just keep it as it is and adapt my questions to accommodate your landscape.

If you're struggling with a particular saying you may want to check that your landscape doesn't have within it the capacity to include any other sayings – might you be a fish on a limb and obviously therefore out of water, or stuck in a rut in a wood you can't see for the trees, or head in the sand and just missed the tide (which is just as well as you might have drowned if you hadn't missed it!)

If at any point you finish a chapter feeling less satisfied than you did at the start you have a few options available to you:

- Return to the original constructed image – you may need to spend some time imagining the landscape you described.
- Continue to make changes to the current landscape until you feel better.
- Imagine the positive anchored memory we discussed at the start of this chapter.
- Do anything that you know shifts you into a more positive frame of mind – listening to a piece of music, exercise, going for a walk, talking to someone.
- Explore what the new landscape has brought up for you non-metaphorically – feelings, thoughts, memories. You are the one who is best able to determine whether you're in a good place to be able to do this. Remember it's not about beating yourself up – just about becoming aware of what is holding you back, and taking steps to release the barriers.

Just to give you a sense of the possibilities, here are a few real-life examples of the LYL process.

"I have a core of me that's confident," said Ben "but I'm not sure it's reached my head yet."

The clue of course lies in the language being used about a "core" of confidence. That is, Ben had an internal representation for his confidence that was a "core". Since it had a description, and was only a construct anyway, playing around with the image of the "core" might enable it to include, rather than exclude, his head?

The Skype call went something like this:

> "How would you describe this core?"
>
> "It's around my stomach."
>
> "And what qualities does the core have?"
>
> "It's like a sun."
>
> "Can you tell me more about this sun?"
>
> "It's yellow, and the beams spread out around my arms, legs and body but stop at my throat."
>
> "What's stopping it from extending beyond your throat?"
>
> "There are clouds in the way."
>
> "What might enable the clouds to move?"

This resulted in much hilarity as we "wooshed" and generally tried different strengths of wind to move the clouds away. Once the clouds were no longer in the way I asked:

> "Can the sun now extend into your head?"
>
> "Yes, a little – it certainly feels warmer."

We then played around with the image until it felt just right, and the sun was streaming through into Ben's head.

Just as we started speaking about the sun streaming, the actual sun here in Scotland (yes, we do get some) started to stream in through my window, and my head on the computer screen developed a halo around it – which helped us further enhance the image for Ben's core of confidence!

My final question was "And how does your confidence feel now?"

"Much better," was the reply.

We then went on to discuss how Ben could keep the image of the streaming sun alive until it became the norm for representing his confidence.

This is really such a great example of why metaphors are so powerful when coaching others. That is, they often bypass the barriers and resistance we have to change, and certainly provide a much less stressful and content-free means of releasing unhelpful thoughts, habits or behaviours.

Another example from a LYL walk in nature involved a wildflower meadow.

Here's a picture from the walk, where Helena's desire to let go of perfection led me to ask her "What part of the current landscape best describes that desire?" I then asked her to walk into that landscape and notice what she noticed.

Although she also had the beach, a park and a wood to choose from, Helena walked into the wildflower meadow that had been left by the groundsman to provide shelter and food for wildlife.

There seemed to be a lot of "Oh, I see" and "That feels better" going on – and over the coming weeks and months, for Helena a different relationship with perfection emerged. One that involved less doing, and more being, and "time for me".

You and I don't need to understand why walking into an area of wild flowers might help us unlock a situation about perfection. I could surmise that because many of the flower heads were now brown, it was a reminder that each was perfect in its own way, in relation to the season and weather. It doesn't really matter what I think though, just what it meant for Helena and that she got insight from the landscape, and insight she could translate into action.

On another walk with a client, Peter, as we walked down a steep path surrounded by trees shared that he was frustrated with the speed with which things were progressing on one of his projects.

I asked him to look around and consider how much of what he could see would have been here less than eight weeks previously. The answer of course was very little of it; the bare trees and perhaps the grass. I'm sure the path ahead would have been illuminated with light from above and not covered in growth. If we'd come here every day for every one of those eight weeks I'm not sure we'd have seen much difference each day. Yet within that time so much had changed.

As you can see, the insights from nature don't have to be big, or only appear when you're looking for them. You can just be walking along and something might come to your attention or to mind. Like the time when I walked along my local beach and noticed the tide:

The water on the Forth was like a millpond – very calm and quiet – and as a result the slow incremental movement of the tide was not noticeable. Which reminded me that often change doesn't come with a big fanfare made in big leaps, but just continual progress every day towards your goal until you realize you've got there.

Which means it's best not to discount even the smallest of hints your subconscious provides when using a landscape to provide guidance on what to do next. If suddenly a thought comes to mind, follow that thought; don't judge it, just see where it takes you and allow for the possibility of solutions to be found and questions to be answered naturally.

One thing to be aware of: the aim is to end up with an amended landscape that represents a less stressed state. As this internal representation changes it can't help but impact and change how you're feeling and thinking. This in turn will impact how you act in the situation.

It can be that simple, but don't underestimate the time it can take until the landscape is "just right". And also remember the mind's capacity to want to retain the current stressed state (and therefore return to the previous landscape) and so trick you into thinking you've cracked it!

Over time and many instances of using this process with myself, and others, I've noticed a difference between those who achieve long-term changes as a result of using the process, and those who find more temporary reprieve.

The difference is in the "completeness" of the landscape they envisage.

If their solution is a stream it seems important to expand the landscape to include the whole life of the stream, from high up in the mountains, through waterfalls, rivers, estuary and into the ocean.

Other times the pattern that needs completing is the time of day – with the landscape needing to run through 24 hours. For others it's the need to represent a whole month, season or even year.

The key is ensuring that what we do makes the situation better, not worse. For example, if someone has spent ages feeling like they're in the dark with no light, then "completing" the pattern isn't likely to be sunrise, sunset and returning to darkness. Completeness, will need to be found in some element within the landscape.

Other patterns of completion may include harvesting the fruits, following the tide from high to low, and so on.

I'm not quite sure yet why this is, but I think it highlights and links to our unconscious connection to nature, something I feel strongly we should be reinforcing, not ignoring or moving away from. If you have any observations I'd love for you to share them. (Although if my recent reliance on a weather app when deciding whether to bring sheets in from the line rather than pay attention to the dark clouds is anything to go by, I have a long way to go myself!)

If we allow nature to be our teacher, then the story of the universe becomes the story of our solar system, which becomes the story of Earth and of humanity and of you and me, and of our flourishing. The next chapter addresses some of the common reactions or resistance experienced by people when using the LYL process. It's a summary of the kind of conversations I've had with clients over the years when dealing with their reactions.

CHAPTER 4

# COMMON REACTIONS TO THE LYL PROCESS

Some people take to the LYL process like a duck to water and embrace its unconventional, quirky and weird nature. They may even try to justify it by saying "It's not weird at all" or "What's quirky about that?"

If you're one of these readers then this chapter isn't really for you. You will already have decided what areas of your life you're going to apply this process to, and be eager to explore it further.

If that's the case, far be it from me to stop you from getting on with using it – why not pop along to Part 2 now and do just that?

After working with people using this process for nearly 20 years what I do know, however, is that it can feel weird for some people. This chapter is more like having me on your shoulder whispering to your inner critic when it says "This won't work," "That's rubbish," "A load of codswallop." I'm not suggesting you can't think it's rubbish, or that you might not find it doesn't work for you. I just want to share with you what's helped others to move to a more open way of thinking about it so you can try it, and potentially maximize the likelihood of moving from being stuck to getting back on track using it.

Later chapters will address what to do if you're stuck, or how to avoid getting stuck in the first place. These situations both assume an understanding of what state you're in currently, a desire to not be stuck and a willingness to do something about it.

The problem is many of us are blissfully unaware we're stuck, or that we're seriously headed in that direction. We're comfortable with the current situation, with no desire to make any changes.

What often happens, therefore, is that we don't make changes until we're already up the creek without a paddle, stuck in a rut or can't see the wood for the trees. We may never have acknowledged previously that we were in a place we didn't want to be; it's only once the pain of being there is too great to handle that we utter the words and decide that we want to take action and do something about it.

We have often, however, been headed in that direction for a long time, and like a captainless ship have been forced onto the rocks by the wind.

Perhaps you can find examples from your own life. Maybe someone you know didn't move jobs until they were made redundant, and yet a few months later they tell you "I wish I'd done it sooner," or someone's marriage ends, much to their surprise and distress, although everyone else can see how much happier they are as a result.

Here I'd like to address how to notice that you may be heading up that creek or towards that rut – and what to do about it.

Sometimes we know we are heading up the creek without paddles or towards a rut. At other times, we might be quite happy and content – or not be happy and content but not consciously know that things need to change.

It comes back to the basics of needing to:

- Know where you want to get to
- Know where you are
- Understand what might be stopping you getting there
- Plot a route
- Take action

The issue is that we often give up on where we want to get to, and put up with where we're at, and find ways of making that as comfy as possible.

I was watching *MasterChef Australia* and one of the contestants, Rose, faced with having to replicate a well-known chef's dish, described herself as being out of her "comfort universe". I loved the expression, and certainly knew what she meant by it.

From a LYL perspective I wondered what insight the phrase might offer.

When we use the term "comfort zone" we're describing a zone within which we're happy to be, with the implication being that there is another zone beyond it where we're uncomfortable, or fearful of being. I'm assuming Rose meant by "comfort universe" that there was a zone even beyond that discomfort zone.

There is of course an interesting observation to be made about this phrase, and it comes from pondering the question – what IS beyond the edge of the universe?

Since scientists don't yet know the answer to that question, and the universe as far as we know is infinite and all that there is, then we **can't** actually operate outside of our "comfort universe". Instead, once we're beyond our comfort zone we're into our infinite comfort universe, and anything and everything is therefore possible within it. Maybe that's why Rose on *MasterChef* accomplished the task.

So, next time you're thinking you're at the edge of your comfort zone, just step happily into your infinite comfort universe, and remember – there is nothing beyond the universe, and therefore any-thing is possible from exactly where you are right now.

Or remind yourself that just when a caterpillar might think its life is over it begins to fly!

How often do we resist change and yet once we get there conclude that it's where we needed to be?

When I was thinking and writing about being out on a limb I realized that once we're describing it as such, we've passed the point of no return – there is no going back. So why do we resist for so long? The aim must be to notice that we've passed this point of no return – and let go. Here's to accepting life as a butterfly.

This also reminds me of my favourite quote, often attributed to the writer Guillaume Apollinaire:

> *"Come to the edge" he said.*
> *They said "We are afraid."*
> *"Come to the edge" he said.*
> *They came. He pushed them.*
> *And they flew.*

And I believe we can all metaphorically fly.

You may think, faced with using metaphor, that you won't know what to say. But no one knows what they're going to say before they say it. In this process there is no right answer and therefore no wrong answer. The answer is whatever comes to mind.

If you can imagine the worst-case scenario in the future, and worry about that happening – you are able to construct images and therefore to use and understand metaphor. And the process asks you to picture and describe the scenario as a landscape – there's lots of prompts in each chapter so you're not starting from scratch with every single saying that you apply to your situation.

If you can describe your situation as one of the sayings then clearly a part of you does know what to say – that part of you has decided which saying was most applicable.

You may also find that a solution emerges as you read the book, or the chapter, that most resonates with you. In that case, you won't need to know what to say!

The above process can seem quite mysterious – the links you make between your situation and the images or scenario that describe them best aren't necessarily obvious or logical.

But we still don't fully understand how our brain works, and this process helps the brain to think differently anyway – some of this process IS mysterious! I can therefore understand if it doesn't feel that logical to you.

There are, though, logical reasons as well as less explicable ones for why this process works – see the chapter on why metaphors work for more on this.

Does everything you do feel logical when you do it? Even the gut feeling? The intuition? The "I'm not sure why I did that but it worked" feeling?

A perfectly natural reaction to applying the process to a situation in your life is fear.

When we're stuck it can often be because we're fearful about the future or goal we've set ourselves. That fear may manifest during this process as a fearful landscape – a clifftop with a steep drop below, or floundering in deep water.

Depending on the level of fear we feel, we may not be able to imagine making any changes to the landscape until we feel safer –

when we come away from the edge or imagine we're floating with a lifejacket on.

Here's what I wrote when I experienced fear in a landscape while writing the book.

As I sit here 1.5 metres from the cliff edge I can feel the fear rising – I'm not even standing up, and yet the fear is still very much apparent.

As I watch the abseilers seemingly show no fear as they walk backwards down the cliff, I realize even they have their safety net – the post hammered into the clifftop to which they've tied their ropes, anchoring themselves for when they drop down the cliff.

I feel safe here on the clifftop because I'm sitting in a chair and know that it and I are going nowhere. I look around for other means of "anchoring", and I see the buoys that anchor the boats, the lifejackets that enable the sailors to float not sink, the wings of birds that allow them to fly not fall and the oil rig's legs that dig deep into the ocean floor for security.

The aim is to anchor yourself to safety so you can then plot a course out from the place of safety.

Be careful where you've placed yourself in relation to what you're scared of – I've just turned my chair round to give my arms and legs some shade from the sun and now have the cliff behind me. It's still the same distance away but the fear has escalated! It has escalated to the point that I'm feeling really apprehensive about moving. I'm not sure how long I can stay facing this direction.

In a less literal clifftop scenario too – when you're faced with any life situation that makes you fearful – you can notice what makes your fear subside and what increases it and do more of one and less of the other.

Remember, it's only from a safe, non-fearful place that your mind is able to access the creative parts of you – if fear is ruling your thought process then you're stuck in fight-or-flight lockdown with no access to logical thinking, just the ability to fight or run away.

The situation may still feel scary, but if you can view it from a non-fearful place you'll be able to see the options available to you much more easily.

## Likely Reactions After You've Applied the Process

The LYL process is very quick, in that you can take a landscape, change its characteristics and within a few minutes feel differently. A little more time to just tease out any remaining niggles and you're there! This can take anywhere between five minutes and an hour or so. Perhaps longer if you decide to use collage, or pictures to help take you on the journey, or if you do it through walking in the landscape – maybe even a day if you then take some time to really describe the end landscape and are working on a particularly meaty challenge.

It's useful to be aware of the potential reactions you may have to applying the process and it making you feel different.

There's a few more things that might happen to you after you apply the LYL process:

> Sally, who has a monthly coaching session with me, rang midweek to say she was stuck. Within five minutes we'd shifted the landscape and hung up to continue her day, perhaps a little more effectively. This despite having called me, just five minutes earlier, in a very stuck state and with no idea what to do.
>
> We have laughed a lot about this since, about both how quickly the situation was turned round and how it enabled her to react and feel much more resourceful.

### Relief/Tiredness/Feeling Emotional

A stuck state can be very stressful and stress means tension. If it's been held for some time then its release is going to feel a relief. Which means you may then feel tired. Think about any situation you've worried about and it's been resolved – often the first reaction is one of relief and relaxation. Perhaps even tiredness.

One client after a very quick but insightful session said she suddenly felt very tired. This was, we decided, a consequence of the constant treading water, the metaphor she had been working with. We agreed she just needed to go with the tiredness and allow her body time to realize that the stressor had been released and to recover.

A good night's sleep may be enough for you to come back at the world firing on all cylinders Or, if the stressful situation has been around for a long time, it may take a little longer to acclimatise to the new state of non-stress. Give yourself some time – cut yourself some slack – be kind to yourself: play/sleep/read/ spend time with friends, alone or with children. Whatever normally allows your mind and body time to renew and revitalize.

The process may have only taken ten minutes but if you're letting go of years' worth of stress, recognize that and honour that stress. Pop a balloon, burn some incense, plant a tree or dig a hole – do whatever you need to metaphorically honour and say goodbye to the stress. It has served its purpose and can now be released.

### Disbelief

Another reaction is disbelief that something so simple can make you feel much better or enable you to understand what to do next. You may start to hunt for the stuckness, feeling as if it's simply hiding from you and waiting to jump out at you in the night when you're not watching.

Trust the process. You represented the situation as A and now, with your metaphor work, you've represented it as B. A didn't allow you to see the solution and B does – we've pulled the curtains back and can now see what has to be done.

If you dwell on, or go hunting for, the stuckness you may just go back to A. You may therefore like to work on making and keeping B the stronger image – for example use a picture that represents B as a screensaver, buy a magazine with pictures that you find supportive or resonant, make a vision board (in reality or on Pinterest).

Do whatever works for you to do to provide the new landscape with some support.

If you catch yourself returning to the old representation, replace it with the new one. If you can go and visit a similar landscape, then do so. The act of visiting a similar landscape seems to work by reminding people that it's a reality – it's possible – and grounding its very energy into their being. It brings it alive in a way an internal vision alone might not be able to do.

### Reverting to How You Saw and Felt about it Before

Yes, this is discussed in the "disbelief" section as an outcome; but it can also be an outcome in its own right, for a number of reasons:

- The new landscape wasn't right – perhaps you still have too many musts, oughts or shoulds. No amount of must can change a landscape into something that motivates you. If you think reverting in this way may be what's hindering your new landscape, think about what the landscape would look like if you let go of the musts and oughts. How would you like the landscape to look?
- The new landscape hasn't been anchored well enough – which means you have a little more time to spend bedding it in so that's it becomes your go-to landscape instead of the one you're leaving behind.
- Some of the other sayings are still in control. Consider which saying now resonates and read that chapter. If this keeps happening, I'd suggest reading all the chapters in sequence.
- We've lost something in B that we treasure in A – we may like a particular tree and we've left it in A, or enjoy the fresh sea air that no longer pervades our new landscape. Aim to ensure that this something is represented in your new antidote landscape.
- Perhaps the situation you were thinking about wasn't something you could control – i.e., perhaps you wanted someone to change rather than changing something within yourself, and the landscape represented the changes you wanted them to make. I'm sorry but that's never going to happen until or unless they want it to – all you can do is support them while they take their own journey.
- Perhaps you don't want the situation now – perhaps it's a long-term aim, and you really want the end result in six months or a year. In which case, what do you need to do to ensure it's still there ready for you when the time is right?

All of this highlights how important it is to understand what situation you're expressing in A, your original landscape.

If you want a goal for a year's time, and the stuck state was more about your impatience – i.e., treading water until it's time – then do revisit the landscape with the impatience as the outcome rather than as the real goal.

- You may just realize you can put your feet down on the sea bed, and enjoy the sea and fresh air and sun while you wait. – What good is swimming out till you're out of your depth, and then treading water waiting!
- You don't believe it will happen because to achieve the goal you think you need more time, more money, more support, better exam results… Don't worry about that for now. Just trust that now the internal landscape has changed, you will notice things, people and resources that will help you achieve your goal.
- Impatience is not ecological or sustainable – envisaging a dam held back by a bridge isn't going to work; nor is hoping the fish mutates overnight and becomes an amphibian, or just replacing one landscape with another without there being a route from one to the other. I'm very happy if this isn't the case for you (there will always be exceptions), but experience has told me that the more realistic a landscape shift the better. It's as if, to enable a second landscape to represent an issue, we need to be able to get there from the first landscape – yes, it's still often quicker than it would be in real life and yes, it is easier to shift through three seasons in five minutes when to do so in reality would take nine months. That said, we've often held our landscape in a particular season for too long anyway – if we'd let the landscape continue to evolve naturally we wouldn't have been stuck in the first place.
- After any process it's useful to identify the first step you will take from this new metaphorical landscape and consider how that action translates into action in the original situation. You are now in a landscape where you are no longer stuck, and understand what you need to do. What do you now realize

you can do – what will you do, when will you do it and do you
need to tell anyone? Do you need to write it down, i.e., how
will you ensure the action takes place – i.e., the sooner the better? if you can do something in the next hour, do it. Within
the next 24 hours is okay too, but any longer than that allows
other commitments, pressures and life in general to get in the
way, and take the energy out of the commitment to take action
towards your goal.

• There ares lots of things that might be getting in the way of
you making progress, which could include: values and what
motivates you, other conflicting goals getting in the way,
adrenaline, negative or unhelpful beliefs, fear, well-being, hormones, an unsupportive physical or emotional environment,
clutter and unhelpful visuals, bullying, and so on. If you think
these might be hindering your progress, there are plenty of
solutions available to mitigate their impact.

Without further ado let's get into Part 2 and start exploring those
sayings, and the landscapes contained within them.

# SAYINGS THAT KEEP US STUCK, AND HOW TO USE THEM TO GET BACK ON TRACK

# CHAPTER 5

# MAKING MOUNTAINS OUT OF MOLEHILLS

This may seem a strange place to start, especially as it's a saying we very rarely use about ourselves. Yet it's that very reason why I'm starting with this saying.

When we're stuck, the mountain we see between ourselves and our goal is very real, very big and often insurmountable. We do not believe we're exaggerating the situation; we firmly *believe* we don't know what to do, and as a consequence believe we're going to be stuck for some time. After all, if the situation was none of these things we'd know what to do and be doing it – right?

Notice I use the word believe. The whole premise of this book is that it's our belief about the situation that is maintaining the state of stuckness. We see the challenge as a mountain, and relate to it as such. All solutions from that perspective therefore require that we climb the mountain, whether we think that's a possibility or not, and every fibre of our being supports that belief.

The Landscaping Your Life (LYL) process shared in this book asks us to revisit our belief that the challenge we're facing is really a mountain. By looking at the situation from many different angles and perspectives it's as if we are able to take the air out of that mountain and deflate it. Or, perhaps we simply need to accept that we're a giant who can traverse the mountain in one step.

We're making mountains out of molehills every time we're stuck. We're waiting for the solution to emerge while looking up at that mountain thinking "How the hell am I ever going to get up there?" We've forgotten that, if we could make the mountain into a molehill, we'd be able to find the solution easily and effortlessly.

Making something more difficult than it really is isn't something to judge ourselves for. It will always feel more difficult until we know the solution and know what to do. The LYL process just helps us get there a little quicker; it provides a short cut, if you will, from mountain to molehill.

It's at this point in many coaching sessions that I get asked "Aren't you suggesting we just need to see life as being full of molehills?"

And my answer is a resounding "No". Going straight to molehills can provide a very monochrome existence.

If life were only full of molehills then we would be not stretching ourselves, not pushing ourselves, not expecting much out of life.

A life full of molehills is about always knowing the answer – which shouldn't be the case.

If we always think we know the answer, how soon before we realize it was really a mountain, and find ourselves clinging to the mountainside with the wind whipping around us, not dressed for the terrain or weather?

If we always think we know the answer how do we learn? Constant knowing and constant molehills is a state of atrophy, unlearning and ultimately death. (Sorry to sound so melodramatic but hopefully you get my drift.)

I'm not therefore suggesting that you only aim for molehills. What I'm recommending is that, even if the challenge you're facing is the size of a mountain, viewing it as a molehill can be useful.

Remember, the LYL process asks us to use a landscape, and take learning from it as if it represents the current situation.

For example, I'm sitting on Kirkcaldy beach in Scotland as I type this, and am surrounded by rock pools. As I look left and right, it looks like I've plonked myself down in the middle of a mini mountain range. I feel a little like Gulliver must have – a giant in a small land. I can see the whole range from start to finish. I am able to easily and effortlessly move around this mountain range to see the pitfalls, passes, valleys and views.

Imagining that these rock pools represent a challenge I'm facing, from this perspective I can see that it's easy to see a route through, and for the journey to feel more manageable.

That's what the LYL process helps us to do – make something that feels too big more manageable.

How often in life, though, do we forget about observing the bigger picture and instead just deal with what's in front of us, forgetting or ignoring the rest of the journey or not even seeing the alternative solutions available to us? Not realizing there may be other, perhaps easier, routes to get to the top of the main summit, and even more options if our objective is really just to get to the other side of the mountain range rather than climb every one!

As I look at the rock pools on the beach I can see clear valleys in between many of the summits, where progress would be quicker and easier, even if it was a longer distance and perhaps less direct. How useful would that be when thinking of a challenge we're facing – to think about the less direct and yet more manageable route?

This is an insight that has already inspired me to send an email to my publisher about this book. Other work commitments mean I'm editing it between training workshops. Workshops that leave me tired and lacking in creativity. As I reflected on the last paragraph I realized asking for an extra week would enable me to walk the route through the valley, and not try to climb the mountain when I'm not prepared for it!

The answer from the publisher came back within minutes, despite it being a Sunday, and in fact gave me another two weeks to finish the editing. How simple to change the situation once I viewed it from a different perspective.

As with all the landscapes, there are always going to be other perspectives and insights that offer additional solutions to be considered. We just need to keep looking.

Another observation from the rock pool mountains in front of me is that one side of the mountain is obviously harder to get up, and the other much easier.

When we're developing action plans in our life it's useful, therefore, to understand which option is harder and which is easier. I'm sure it's not just me who can get carried away with taking action, and making progress, without thinking through the consequences. Wouldn't it be preferable to think about our goal and the criteria for achieving the goal, and then assessing the options using these criteria?

In my book editing example, the goal is an edited manuscript. The main criterion is how well the words have been edited. The options are to meet the agreed deadline but suffer stress as I take no time off after training and just get my head down to the editing work, or ask for some additional time so I can have some downtime to allow me to access a more creative mindset.

Looking at the rock pools also reminds me of the potential benefit of developing a 3D representation of the goal/challenge we're facing.

As with any of the LYL techniques, it's always more effective to stick with the metaphor before delving back into the actual real-life situation. With this particular saying that therefore means you should, either in your imagination or in sand or soil, mould the metaphorical mountain range that best represents the challenge you're facing. To do that you'll already have to make it molehill size or smaller, which can't help but provide a different point of view to help you understand what you're missing, and what is the best route through.

Once you've completed your 3D representation the key is to observe the patterns. You may for example notice that your mountain defies gravity, or isn't really mountain-shaped, or is too big for its surroundings, or has too-straight contours.

The beauty of a 3D representation is that you can then remould it and ensure that it does align with gravity, or is mountain-shaped, or does have appropriate contours. As you do this remoulding you may notice that your relationship to the situation changes. Perhaps solutions come to mind as your sandy hands score a path into your mountainside.

If you're unable to make a 3D representation you may want to try a 2D version.

On a recent workshop a group were asked to draw the challenge they were wishing to resolve. Drawing it metaphorically as a mountain range, just as we found with the 3D mould, helps keeps us away from the real-life detail that is often the reason why we're still stuck. Exploring the problem as if it's a mountain range allows us to explore the challenge without the excuses, musts, oughts and shoulds. It allows us to see the patterns that are the reason why we're stuck, and then to make changes to release those unhelpful patterns.

The group in question had drawn lots of smaller hills surrounding one huge mountain. On reflection they noticed that the mountain looked more like a triangle, with straighter sides than a real mountain would ever have. I therefore suggested they draw the larger mountain to look more lifelike.

While this edited mountain didn't change in size, its sides became more sloped and less angular; as they made these changes someone added a winding path to the top. As someone else got a green pen and started filling in the mountain they said "Perhaps we've got this all wrong – rather than them being resistant to our suggestions perhaps this person just wants what's best for the organization, and hasn't heard enough to know that's what we want too." This resulted in them developing a very different communication plan to the one they'd been using, and a plan that they felt might just resolve the issue.

If they'd discussed the problem without reference to the metaphor they may of course have identified the need for an alternate communication plan. What using the mountain metaphor allowed them to do though was put their annoyance and judgement about the other person to one side. The belief in their own rightness of action was toned down as they represented the challenge and simply noticed what they noticed about what they had drawn.

The metaphor allowed them to give themselves advice about the most appropriate course of action to take.

While 3D and 2D representations are helpful, exploring a real landscape will provide additional ideas and suggestions.

As I watch the kids currently playing in the rock pool I notice they're not going up and over the rocks, but round or through the water. They're small and know their limitations, and don't feel the need to prove anything to anyone. They're just having fun, and running around and exploring the rock pools with their buckets and spades. For them it's about the pools, not the mountains.

Some older boys were obviously thinking the same. They just walked past – walking along the ridges – but only to get from one rock pool to another. No big aim, just exploring the range of pools and all that they contain.

They've been told to be quiet by their mother, who worries they're bothering me.

Isn't that what rock pools are for though – exploring? How can I get annoyed when children are being children, and I've chosen to sit in the middle of an ideal play area for them, rather than watch from the edge of the beach with all the other adults!

Perhaps your mountain needs to be more playful, or the focus needs to be on the water, not the surrounding mountains. Or maybe it's about sitting at the edge and letting someone else do the exploring for you.

Remember, being too quick to say "That suggestion won't work" invalidates the usefulness of the metaphor. We already think we're out of good ideas. Shooting additional ideas down before they've had chance to grow and morph will just keep you where you are currently – stuck. Getting back on track requires our thinking to be loosened and expanded, not constrained by overly negative thinking too early in the process.

As I have said many times and will say again, there's no right or wrong with metaphors – just tangents and ideas your mind notices as a result of exploring the metaphor – tangents that may hold the kernel of a solution within them. You just need to be vigilant in following the clues.

As I look down I notice another mini mountain range, in the sand – the undulations made by the tide as it moves in and out across the beach and weaves through the rock pools, leaving small indentations in the sand. Some still have water trapped in them as the tide retreats.

Of course, these sandy mountains are even smaller than molehills, and are not as permanent as even those easily squashed soil-made hills. I can stand on one until I ruin its form. Isn't that what many of our problems are like? We act as if they're made of rock and immovable, when in fact they're malleable, able to be altered and improved easily.

Imagining my issue as a mountain might have had me heading for the mountains to get some insight, or into the fields of my youth hunting for molehills. However, sitting here, thinking I'm going to be writing about tides or the ocean, I'm in fact noticing more about molehills and mountains – so much more than I could by exploring it solely in my imagination.

It's as if we're taking the metaphorical landscape in our head out into nature, and if metaphors are worth a million words then nature is infinite in its ability to provide meaning, whatever intention we started out with.

Thus far, we have assumed that what's keeping us stuck is a mountain, and once we can resolve it and find the solution we will have made it into a molehill.

What about the molehills we talk ourselves into believing are mountains?

I've got arthritic knees, and after the most effective personal training session in years, I started to make mountains from my personal fitness molehills. The evidence in front of me was that things were improving, and yet there I was worrying about what if my knees hurt tomorrow, or that it was a fluke and I'd soon be back to suffering from painful knees.

Fears are one way in which we make our mountains bigger than they need to be (molehills too).

As they say, fears are simply False Expectations Appearing Real.

- Fears about what others think
- Fears of failure
- Fears of things going wrong

By all means do a risk assessment, but understand these expectations are just that – expectations, fuelled by fear rather than reality.

Don't we do that a lot in life – worry about a future that there is no evidence to suggest we're headed for. It's as if when we're not actually faced with a mountain we manufacture one.

That said, when we're stuck, all we've forgotten is that we're facing a mountain (real or imagined) and simply need to find a way to get over it, thereby making it a molehill.

The rest of this part of the book looks at some of the other sayings we use to describe being stuck (the mountains we're moulding in our mind) and examines numerous ways of making them much more manageable molehills.

We'll be starting with being stuck in a rut, because without a sense of get-up-and-go we're never going to take any action to resolve a challenge we're facing.

# CHAPTER 6

# STUCK IN A RUT

A suit-wearing management team were walking up a single-track country lane surrounded by high, overgrown hedges. It was the middle of the countryside in southern England, and they were on a vision-setting day discussing the future for their organization.

"The problem is, if we're not careful and we keep doing what we've always done, just like this lane we'll peter out."

"Yes, we're stuck in a rut," someone else replied as they looked down the lane, towards the seeming dead end further along, with grass growing in the middle of it.

As they all nodded their heads someone noticed a small hole in the hedge, and said:

"To get out of this rut we need to do something different – like go through that hole."

Five minutes later, after they'd all pushed their way through the hedge and dusted themselves down, they stood in the middle of an expansive green field at the top of a small hill, looking at the landscape all around them.

"That's better – no paths already decided, no direction already plotted, just an open field ready for us to make plans about!"

When the management team got back into the boardroom the vision they identified for the organization was certainly more innovative and creative than might have been imagined before the walk.

In this instance, a walk around the real landscape provided a different perspective on the current challenge they were facing.

They could have found the solution by imagining they'd taken themselves on the walk, and noticing what came to mind. The benefit of this real-life situation was that they all made the observations together, and jointly made the decision to walk through the hole. It was much easier to make plans thereafter, knowing they had a shared vision for where they wanted to go and, just as importantly, agreement that they were leaving behind the rut-like lane and all that it represented.

Following in the management team's footsteps might work for you. Try following this five-step process:

- Find a rut
- Stand in the rut
- Step out of the rut
- Notice what you notice about the situation
- Be surprised by what you discover

And yes, it can be that simple – the mind does work in mysterious ways!

Perhaps it seems a little simplistic; however, if you think about it, that is the metaphorical solution:

If you're in a rut, get out of it.

Even if getting out of the rut doesn't prove as easy as following the five steps above, though, you will find some way to get out of it. Standing in a rut is no fun, and sooner or later a solution will emerge that will enable you to break free. Even if you have to wait for hunger, thirst or some other discomfort to provide the motivation to find a solution to get out of there.

Trust me, if we can easily break free of a real rut in the landscape, we can certainly break free of the ruts of our imagination.

Before we start diving into ruts, if you've a situation that feels like you're in a rut about, then now is the time to consider the type of metaphorical rut you're in. The questions raised and insights shared can then be applied by you to your own personal rut.

Consider a situation you're stuck about, and as you do so bring to mind an image of the rut in relation to that situation.

Perhaps more than in most of the other chapters, it's important here that you keep the real-life situation at the back of your mind rather than the forefront, and answer the following questions from the perspective of being "stuck in a rut" in a metaphorical way rather than focusing on whatever the ins and outs are of your particular situation, i.e., please stay with the metaphor, and **don't** allow the brain to distract you with "But that won't work," "I've tried it before," "It's their fault I can't do anything to change it, not mine", and so on. That willotherwisw keep you stuck.

Let's get started – first check that the internal voice that might be suggesting this is a little weird has been turned down and then consider what your answers would be to the following questions about your particular rut.

- What's the rut like – depth, width, length, shape, soil type?
- What's stuck in the rut – your foot or feet, arm, head, body?
- What's the weather and temperature around the rut? Further afield?
- What about the surrounding landscape – sky, trees, fields, plants, sounds?
- What's stopping you from getting out of the rut?
- What happens when you envisage stepping out of the rut?

Now reflect on the original real-life situation you wanted to get out of. Has this exploration shifted anything? Have any actions you could take come to mind?

Please remember, this doesn't have to make sense from a logical perspective. I'd go so far as to say: give yourself permission to not need to understand it logically. At some level, because you can relate to the words "stuck in a rut", some part of your subconscious does really understand the situation in terms of those words.

For example, I might ask you to describe the weather by your rut, and you answer "It's raining," without knowing why. Yet before you know it, your mind has taken you on a journey: from a rainy day and sticky mud, to noticing the rain stop and the sun come out; the rain starts to be absorbed by the ground, the hot sun helps evaporate the rain, what was stuck now feels free and movement out of the rut is possible.

Someone else may not even get a sense of the journey at all – they may simply realize they feel or are thinking differently about the situation, and that a solution or solutions have emerged.

As we discovered in Chapter 2, metaphors are a great way to tap into the power of the subconscious. A subconscious that has the solutions that may be hiding from our conscious awareness. The priority is finding the solution, not getting too worried about why the process worked.

Further options to help find a solution from within the rut-like landscape might include:

- Exploring the imagined landscape some more.
- Making changes to the image you have of your rut.
- Imagining moving from the current landscape into a new one that doesn't contain a rut.
- Playing around with the saying and getting a little absurd (hint: you might instead not be able to see the mud for the rut, or simply be stuck up or in a tree).

If you think this may be helpful to you at this time you'll find more guidance about how to do this in Part 3.

For most of us being stuck in a rut is a minor level of stuckness. After all, if you've noticed that you're stuck in a rut, you just need to step out and get back on track.

If you're reading this and thinking that you're still feeling stuck, there may be other things going on:

- You've not noticed you are in a rut (in which case you may want to read the head in the sand chapter first).
- You get distracted very easily.
- You've got caught in a vicious circle of constantly being in a rut, and it's not particularly related to just the current situation, and not only in one area of your life.
- You're more than just stuck in a rut.

## You Get Distracted Very Easily

It's funny how easy it is to live the chapter I'm writing. After being very focused while writing other chapters, I found myself very distracted while writing this one. I realized that's what happens when we're stuck in a rut – we realize we're stuck, decide to do something about it but, before we take that step out, get sidetracked and just keep walking in the rut. After all, a rut is very easy to get out of – so why haven't we got out of it yet? Because it's also very comfortable and easy to stay in. There are no decisions to be made; you just walk where the rut takes you.

Sticking with the metaphor for a moment, consider your answer to the following:

- What are the distractions – perhaps they're other parts of the landscape, or what's round the corner (see Alison Smith Landscaping Your Life YouTube playlist for a vlog on the subject of turning a corner), or what you can hear, or who you're with?
- How could you keep more focused on the rut, and getting out of it?
- What changes could you make to the landscape to make it less distracting?
- What would enable you to keep focused on the task in hand?

The aim throughout this chapter is to step out of the rut and get back into the flow, whether you're doing that metaphorically or you actually go and find a rut to get into and then out of. Then it's just about noticing what happens next!

## Vicious Circle of Stuck in a Rut

If you've been in a rut for a while it's much more likely that the question is: what's stopping you from leaving the rut?

If it's things to do with the landscape, i.e., the mud is very thick and gloopy, or you've got your ankle caught, or it's too steep or big a rut, then it's important that you metaphorically find solutions to these challenges, which in turn will help you break free of the rut and get back on track.

It could be that you like ruts, and may need to explore more about what being in a rut gives you. The important question here is "How do I get what I enjoy about being in a rut from a reality/landscape that doesn't have any ruts?"

For example, if being in a rut gives you a well-deserved rest, it's important that any solution includes plenty of opportunity to rest; if being in a rut provides you with a great view of the landscape then it's important to ensure a great view is included in the final-outcome landscape.

If the answer to what's stopping you is lack of energy and enthusiasm, then you could try sticking with the metaphor a little longer and asking:

- What will provide me with the motivation to get out of the rut?
- How can I get more energy to get out of the rut?

I think, however, in this situation going to the non-metaphorical antidote might also be needed. Because it's all about finding motivation to take action in the direction of your goal.

What's stopping you might include:

- Your lack of motivation
- Negativity
- Other conflicting goals getting in the way
- Abused adrenaline
- Negative or unhelpful beliefs
- Fear
- Not-so-well-being
- Hormones – and that's not just an age or female thing either!
- Unsupportive physical environment
- Unsupportive emotional environment
- Bullying – from self or others

If you think any of these may be getting in the way the internet is a wonderful resource to help find potential solutions. You may also find some possible solutions on my Landscaping Your Life blogs and video blogs. They're certainly topics I revisit often.

If I can offer a personal perspective on this, I recently spent time watching an inspirational TV channel rather than my normal choice and realized the saying "We are what we eat" could be expanded to "We are what we eat, read, watch, listen to and who we spend time with." It's important to consider how our other actions might be supporting us staying in a rut.

Just continuing with the metaphor a little longer, compare the answer someone stuck in a rut versus someone not stuck in a rut would give to the following questions:

- What time do you go to bed?
- How much sleep do you get?
- What do you read?
- What do you watch?
- Who do you spend time with?
- Who do you avoid spending time with?
- What do you eat more of?
- What do you eat less of?
- How do you start your day?

- How do you finish your day?
- What do you do daily that inspires you?
- Do you know what you want from life?
- Do you know what motivates you – and do you do these things often?
- Do you know what demotivates you – and do you avoid these things?

The key is realizing what action you now need to take to ensure you get out of the rut – and stay out.

## You're More Than Just Stuck in a Rut

Unlike the other sayings, you may find that "stuck in a rut" is only a partial description of the current situation. We certainly can hide behind stuck in a rut when the situation is really bigger, or more difficult, than we've described. I don't want to make that the case if you really are just stuck in a rut, but I feel it's only right to address this here.

When you consider being stuck in a rut I'd like you think about:

- How long have you been stuck?
- What is stuck, what can you move and what can't you move?
- How are you stuck – i.e., what's stopping you from moving?

Remember we're still talking metaphorically here – no slipping back into the real-life situation. Stick with the image you have of the rut and the surrounding landscape and, if you have one, the destination landscape you'd like to get to.

Having answered the above questions, how would you now describe the situation?

- Trapped in a rut
- Stuck in a hole
- Stuck in the mud
- Bogged down
- Between a rock and a hard place

- Going round in circles – in which case see Chapter 12
- Another description

Spend a few moments thinking about which of these is most appropriate, as it will determine the effectiveness of the process. Once you've determined which saying best describes the situation, ask questions of that saying – questions such as:

- Trapped – what do you need to do to get free? Do you need any tools to do that or any help?
- Hole – how can you fill the hole in?
- Mud – how do you get the mud out? Can you change the mud to water?
- Bogged down – by what?
- Between a rock and a hard place – follow the process outlined in Chapter 3 to change this alternative internal image.

Basically, explore what you need to do to get unstuck. And then imagine doing it – i.e., change the internal image/representation to a more helpful and less stuck one – one where you're leaving being stuck behind you.

As it's seemingly such a simple solution, you may want to imagine running the solution for a little while to notice if you slip back into the rut again.

If you do slip back, you may need to ask:

"What do I need to do to ensure I don't fall back into this, or other, ruts in the future?"

For example, you may need to imagine filling the rut in, or putting a net or planks over it. If you're going to be filling the rut in, what will you fill it in with – soil, water, cement, a plant or tree or something else entirely? You may even want to imagine the kind of warning sign the highways department would put up to warn people about the rut. Or you might want to paint your very own warning sign in vivid colours that has people take note.

Just keep making changes to the metaphorical and imagined rut until it looks, feels and sounds different, and until it's no longer a rut that you can get stuck in.

As you've been thinking about ruts you may have noticed that solutions to the real-life situation have started to emerge, and you feel positive about being able to get back on track.

Once out of the rut you may find that you're easily back on track – or you may find that you're not quite fully unstuck, even if you have left the rut behind. The next chapter will help you with any stuckness still left and to see the wood, when you currently can't see the wood for the trees.

# CAN'T SEE THE WOOD FOR THE TREES

Jen rang me one day in a panic. "I just don't know what to do, it's all got too much for me," she said.

Over the years, Jen has been introduced to many of the unconventional tools I use in coaching. This call was prompted by a feeling of escalating panic, and an inner knowing that the calm she craves is often on the other side of using one of these tools.

"The problem is, I need to feel better now. I don't have time for lots of thinking, pondering or soul-searching – please help!"

At the time I was writing the contents page of this book. I asked her to listen as I read out all the chapter headings, and let me know which one best reflected how she was feeling.

"Can't see the wood for the trees, definitely," she replied.

For the next few minutes I asked her to describe the wood and trees she was imagining. As with any metaphorical exploration, some questions make more sense than others.

When I asked her how many trees there were, she replied "It's like a forest. There's loads of them."

"The phrase isn't can't see the forest for the trees," I was a little surprised to find myself saying.

"What happens if you make the forest into a wood?" I asked next.

"Oh! The trees change into beech trees," she replied, and then continued: "Oh my God, that's brilliant. I know what I've got to do – must dash – thanks," and hung up!

Even I was surprised at the speed of the shift in perspective, and the abrupt way the call came to an end.

If I think about it for a moment, though, I shouldn't have been surprised.

Jen was headed for a deadline, and if she'd known what to do she would not have had time to call me. She'd have just been getting on with what she knew she needed to be doing. Being stuck meant she wasn't engaged with any activity, just wrapped up in a sense of stuckness. She was certainly seeing the problem as an unclimbably huge mountain towering above her.

If I'd asked Jen about the problem there's every chance she'd have spiralled down into describing the problem even more, with the potential of getting even more stuck.

By using the metaphor we were able to give Jen a moment's break from the real-life situation. A break in which her subconscious was able to offer a suggestion. A suggestion that in the metaphor meant changing the type of tree being envisaged. That shift in perspective allowed a door to be opened in her mind, and it was a door to a solution for her problem.

Obviously once that solution came to mind, and her sense of stuckness was released, the deadline took over as she realized what she needed to do to meet it.

Jen and I still laugh at the brevity of that call, which must have been no more than five minutes, and the abruptness of its ending. I still don't know why the type of tree made the difference, nor what changing it allowed her to understand. I just trust that it worked for her and she knew what she had to do, when five minutes earlier she didn't.

Until starting to write this chapter I'd never thought about it before, but this saying can have two meanings:

- Can't see the detail (the wood it's made of) of one tree for all the other trees. Not usually what we mean when we use this phrase, but we shouldn't discount it until we've explored the different meanings – solutions, can come from the most unexpected and interesting of directions, after all.

- Can't see the small forest (i.e., wood) for the trees – so busy with all the detail I can't see the bigger picture; perhaps it even suggests being a little like a "headless chicken" running round in circles.

I'm going to concentrate on the first meaning – too busy noticing all the trees and can't see the bigger picture.

To get the most from this chapter it makes sense to have a "problem" you can relate "can't see the wood for the trees" to. The exploration and questions asked on the following pages will certainly make more sense if you do this, rather than if you're simply reading the chapters sequentially.

Take a little time to bring to mind a stuck situation you'd like some clarity on, that you could use this description about.

How satisfied do you feel with the current situation – on a scale of 0–10?

Now please put the situation you're wanting insight on to the back of your mind, as if you're filing it away in your pending tray to go back to later.

Bring to mind the wood you can't see because of the trees. I know it may feel a little strange but trust me, you will have an answer – either because you can construct an image or because you can just intuitively give one.

Trust it will, and does, make sense to your mind.

As you imagine the wood consider your answers to the following questions. Remember not to think too deeply – it's not a test, and no one is listening. It's simply an exploration of the metaphor you're using to describe a situation. Don't wonder what your responses mean in reality, or why you even have an answer at all. Just continue to answer the questions as if it's the most natural thing in the world to be able to do.

- Describe the trees – their type, size and shape, the size and shape of their leaves, the colours, the textures.
- Describe any sounds you can hear.
- Describe what you can feel – wind, temperature.
- Describe as much of the trees and the wood as you can see.

Don't be surprised or worried if you can't answer all of these questions – it depends on how much of a wood you can see, and what's stopping you from seeing it. They're simply prompts to allow you to understand how much of a perspective you can obtain if you look a little more closely:

- What is stopping you from observing the wood rather than getting distracted by the trees?
- How big is the wood?
- Are there paths and boundaries?
- Do you know what's round the corner, over the hill or at the bottom of the hill?
- What else could you do to view the wood better?
- Is there anything else it's useful to notice?

In other words, explore the wood and trees in such a way that means you perhaps can now see the wood for the trees. You might want to try:

- Going into the imagined wood and walking through it, around it, away from it and/or viewing it from above or below.
- Filling in the gaps in your picture, using what you know about woods, to make it clearer.
- Being within it – at one with the wood (there is no right or wrong, remember).

As I said to Jen, the saying doesn't say "can't see the forest for the trees", which means we're talking about a relatively small number of trees. It's usually forests that are miles from anywhere, while woods are generally on the edge of villages or towns – which means help and support are not too far away either.

- Does knowing there is a village or town nearby help?
- Or perhaps it's about making it a wood in the middle of nowhere or even making it into a forest.
- As you imagine the wood, where is it in relation to you – all around you, in front of you or behind you? What happens if you change your relationship to the vision? Perhaps try stepping into it and associating with it (being in the landscape), or disassociating yourself from it and viewing it as if you were holding a picture of the trees/wood.

Don't forget we also have the ability to move around the landscape and explore it. To find out about the characteristics of the wood.

- What's hidden behind the tree immediately in front of you?
- Why did you come to the wood in the first place?

Sometimes when we're on a walk we decide to take a short cut through a wood; if we then get lost in it, the issue becomes how to find our way back out – we may tend to forget our original reason for going on the walk.

- What's the underlying goal here? Is the current situation part of the solution or simply a distraction?
- Can you get to your destination without going through the wood?

Before moving on, reflect on the current real-life situation – how does it feel? Maybe you're already becoming unstuck, or are even back on track already? On a scale of 0–10 how satisfied do you feel now?

If you still have room for improvement you now have a few options:

- Explore the imagined landscape some more.
- Go and visit a real-life wood.
- Make changes to your imagined trees and wood.
- Imagine moving from the current landscape into a new one.

- Play around with the saying and get a little absurd with it (see Part 3 for more on this, which might include not being able to see the see the fish for the water, or not feeling the wood for the trees).

Let's consider these options somewhat further.

## Explore the Imagined Landscape Some More

You might want to draw it, get your children involved or meditate on or in it. Anything to bring it to life and help you to "see" the wood.

Perhaps a map would help? The question then is what type of map – after all one used to drive from A to B will be very different in the detail it provides from one where you walk from A to B.

Other times it may mean making a collage – either of the situation or of the landscape –of the current situation and/or of the desired state. It won't make sense to others but might help you make sense of the situation, and more importantly the options available.

For example, the collage on this page provided some insight to a situation where I couldn't see the wood for the trees. Oddly, it was adding the feeling of walking in bare feet on the moss that changed how I was relating to the situation. That doesn't have to make sense

to you, but it did to me at the time. Imagining walking in bare feet on moss provided more of a sense of openness, and released the sense of urgency that was stressing me, and therefore stopping me from seeing the options that were available to me. A more relaxed state of body, facilitated by bare feet on moss, calmed my mind, and allowed me to access that more creative part of me.

Remember there's no right or wrong – we're just exploring the situation as a metaphor, as trees in a wood, rather than in reality.

## Go and Visit a Real-life Wood

And just walk around it and notice what you notice. Notice how the following images I took on a recent trip – may alter your perception of your wood, or suggest some changes you might want to make to your constructed landscape.

The benefit of you going on the walk rather than using my suggestions is that you will notice what you need to notice that makes sense of your interpretation of the landscape. I can only provide examples and hope they trigger a response that helps you shift the current stuck state.

If you go for a walk, notice the difference when you walk further into the wood.

My thoughts are: All there is are trees everywhere you look. If asked what is a wood from here – you'd start to detail the different trees and plants and even animals that make up the wood. You wouldn't know the size of it, nor the shape of it, nor its surroundings but you would be able to provide information about what the wood was made up of.

The phrase of course suggests that we've lost sight of the wood in the process of cataloguing every tree and we know every footpath, fern and fairy glen. I'd suggest we might have got lost in there – forgotten about our objective or goal. Remind me again – why did we come into the wood in the first place?

We might therefore start with considering your objective for being in the wood. Why is it important to be in the wood in the first place? Understanding the why will help you plot a course out – after all, the route will be very different depending on the answer:

- To get to the other side
- To get to the centre
- To spend time in a wood
- To understand the wood
- To change the wood
- To flatten the wood
- To enhance the wood

The clue is in the saying – it's about the wood, not the trees. Don't let yourself be distracted; keep focusing on the wood.

## Make Changes to Your Imagined Trees and Wood

Unless exploring the landscape has helped you realize you weren't really stuck, it's likely you'll have to imagine making changes to your landscape.

To do that, bring to mind your original image of the trees. You may notice that some subtle or not-so-subtle changes have already taken place – what other changes might you want to make to that image?

There's a checklist of ways that the landscape could be changed in Part 3.

Some initial suggestions might be:

- Change the type of trees.
- Make them further or closer apart.
- Cut some branches out; make the colours brighter or more muted or add more or less colour.
- Imagine the trees with or without movement.
- Imagine louder or softer sounds or make your mental image of the wood bigger or smaller. Or perhaps see it from a different perspective, or at a different time of day or year, or when it's cooler or warmer.
- If you can't "see" the wood perhaps it's because the sounds are too loud, or the weather is too distracting.
- Muting them might therefore help with the "seeing", the aim being to make changes until it feels, looks or sounds just right.

Don't forget: all Jen had to do was change the type of trees to beech – that made all the difference and inspired immediate action.

In other words, play around with the image. Since the original image depicts a stuck state, it follows that making changes will enable you to get unstuck.

Another option is to find a picture of a landscape that depicts the current stuck state and make the changes you feel like making to it, by cutting the picture up and adding other images to it, making it into more of a collage. For example, perhaps change the sky, add a tree or take one out, change the flowers or grass. Keep going until the new landscape feels, or looks, or you just know is, right. Put it somewhere visible or even make it into a screensaver. Do whatever enables you to be reminded of this new landscape – a landscape that represents moving forward and being back on track.

Once you've finished playing around with the landscape, it's important to reflect on the original situation.

- Has something changed; does the situation feel, look or sound better?
- What actions in the current situation or different perspectives have come to mind as you've reviewed the images or made the changes?
- What will your first step be – and when will you take it?
- How satisfied do you feel now about the situation on a scale of 0–10?

Remember that if you procrastinate too much longer the wood may just become like these trees.

Unless of course that's the solution?

Something to note: the process can be used time and time again when you're in varying states of stuckness, and applied to any situation in your life. If you revisit a saying for a second time, remember the situation you're applying it to is different, and therefore so may be the solution. Each time you revisit a saying, therefore, it's important that you answer the questions again, noticing what differences there are this time.

Often, once you can see the wood for the trees, it's very easy to get back on track and head for your desired outcome. Sometimes, however, you may then feel like you're up the creek without a paddle.

The next chapter helps you to find your paddle and get out of the creek.

# CHAPTER 8

# UP THE CREEK WITHOUT A PADDLE

I was walking along a creek with Doug, a colleague from work, after he'd said he resonated with this saying.

As we explored, using his own representation of the landscape, he was very resolute that he wanted to progress without a paddle.

We explored the impact of that decision – he knew where he was headed, and said he'd prefer to get out, scramble up a cliff and drag the boat past an intersection to keep it headed in the right direction without the use of a paddle.

I was curious as to why he was so sure the answer was not to look for a paddle.

His response was that the paddle represented making progress with other people and he wanted to do it on his own.

The problem was he'd jumped too soon to realizing he thought the paddle was other people telling him what to do. No matter how hard I tried to demonstrate how difficult it was to be in a boat without a paddle, he wasn't prepared to budge from "I don't want a paddle" – even though the saying would certainly lead us to conclude that it's this lack of a paddle that is at least contributing to our current predicament!

One solution was to get an engine – which, although noisy, did give him the ability to move through the landscape under his own steam, so to speak. I can't help but feel, though, that if he'd fully put the situation to the back of his mind and gone with the flow of the process we might have discovered a more eloquent solution.

A reminder therefore to keep with the metaphor – to answer the questions from the perspective of the landscape.

If you jump in too soon wondering what the paddle is, or what represents the water, or whatever, you'll reduce the effectiveness of the process. If you switch back too soon, the barriers you've put up to finding a solution (in the example above, not wanting other people's help) or barriers to changing what you're doing, will rear their ugly heads. If you stick with the metaphor those barriers won't even exist, making solutions much easier to observe.

Let's worry about what it means later on once we've identified a solution within the landscape.

You could just jump straight to my own observations, which, in this chapter more than most, may give you a solution without you having to work on your own relationship to the saying.

However, if the saying really does resonate then it's preferable for you to explore the landscape you're relating to before adding in my interpretations.

As with every other chapter, double-check that this is the saying that best describes how you're feeling about a situation you'd like some insight on.

I remember someone choosing "up the creek without a paddle" as the saying that best represented the challenge they were facing, and us having a lot of problems trying to describe the metaphor. It felt as if we'd picked this saying too consciously, and perhaps one of the other sayings and metaphors might have described better the over-arching situation and made more sense.

Just double-check that this saying really does best describe the challenge you're wanting insight on. If it does, after determining how satisfied you are with the current situation on a scale of 0–10, put the situation to the back of your mind and bring your attention to the saying:

Up the creek without a paddle.

The aim is to firstly explore the landscape so that you understand your predicament a little more. To do that you may want to draw it – those I work with find that drawing always helps, but particularly when they're up a creek! It's as if seeing where they are in relation to everything else helps plot a course out.

Questions you may want to ask yourself include:

- What can you see? Look through all 360 degrees – forward, back, up and down, etc.
- Where are you – in the water, in a boat of some description?
- What sort of boat are you in?
- Describe the creek – size, shape, surroundings, routes in and out.
- Describe the water – depth, temperature, movement, colour, clarity, buoyancy, flow direction; is it tidal?
- Where is the paddle – did you have one and lose it? Or perhaps you never had one.
- Is the paddle your only source of momentum and/or steering?
- Is it that you're up a creek that's the problem, or rather being paddleless?
- What is at the end or start of the creek?
- In what direction does the water flow?

Continue with your exploration of the creek:

- Where do you want to be (not always a question I ask so soon, but when up the creek it feels very relevant to being able to plot a course out) – can you point in the desired direction?
- What's between you and your destination?
- What's stopping you heading for that destination?
- What would you need to do to head for that destination?

A lot of LYL sessions I've done have involved the tide and the impact that a different time of day and therefore tide can have on a situation. One time the estuary was full of water when we started our work, and at the end of the session the water was a trickle in the middle of the mudflat! It perfectly represented what we'd worked on during the session: if the creek is tidal, there's an awful lot of movement that can take you back either into the flow or on to dry land without the need for a paddle.

I wrote some of this chapter out in a landscape, and I was amazed at how what once looked like a little creek at the edge of the UNESCO world heritage site of the Forth Bridge no longer looked like a creek; the tide had come in beneath its imposing granite piers and the creek was now simply part of the Forth River.

Simply by understanding more about the current situation, even if only metaphorically, you may find that the original situation already feels different – where are you on the satisfaction scale of 0–10?

If there's still some room for improvement, then other options are for you to:

- Explore the imagined landscape some more.
- Go and visit a real-life creek if possible.
- Make changes to your imagined paddles/creek scenario (see Part 3 for more on these).
- Imagine moving from the current landscape into a new one.
- Play around with the saying and get a little absurd (see Part 3 for more on this – it might include being up a tree without a paddle, which I hope you agree would be a different predicament entirely).

Here's what would be my response if I was really physically up the creek without a paddle. Perhaps it suggests a solution that you can more easily apply directly to the real-life situation without having to try too hard to translate the metaphor. See what you think.

Imagine for a moment what being up the creek without a paddle would really feel like. For example, I always imagine steep cliff walls surrounding me, and whirlpools making it even more difficult to make any progress. What does your creek look, sound and feel like? Any treacherous waters? Rocks obstructing the course?

Whenever I use this saying I also always imagine still being in the boat, rudderless due to the lack of a paddle. The following solution therefore comes from that perspective; but the solutions would be very different if you were in the water. For example, you might then need a life ring, towel and firm ground. A very different solution to the one you're just about to read. If you do feel as if you're in the water, you may want to spend a little time considering what to do to get back into the boat, or develop your own seven-step process to get back on track. You can, of course, also identify a process for getting back on track for any of the other sayings.

The seven steps in my own personal antidote are:

- Stop!
- Life Jacket
- Mission
- Guides and Travellers
- Map
- Compass
- Paddle

You may find as you look at the list of steps above that you've already taken the first few, and you're just stuck at one of the steps in the middle.

One thing to remember and be aware of. When you're in either of the first two steps it's not as easy to get going. I know, because I did a bit of method writing when I first developed this seven-step process. Friends kept asking how long until I got to writing about the mission as I had become very negative. You may therefore need to ensure you persevere to ensure you get on to step three.

## STOP!

Think about it. If we're drifting aimlessly, or even going round in circles, until we stop we can't really plot a route out, or even understand what's happening. We're at the mercy of external forces.

If you're in the boat, there are going to be a number of different ways to stop. You may have an anchor, although it's unlikely and you may have to ground yourself. On the other hand, you may be able to moor or tether the boat.

STOP! is about finding a means of giving yourself breathing space to assess the situation. It's about grounding ourselves with the intention of being able to then act from a place of calm and peace, not from a place of fear. It's certainly easier to make decisions when we're calm compared to in a state of panic.

## Life Jacket

Once we've stopped it is possible that we could move straight on to defining our mission and deciding who our fellow guides and travellers are going to be. Many people do that, and do manage to get out of the creek. However, as soon as the going gets rough and their confidence gets dented, many soon end up back up the creek. They don't have the confidence to stay out there in the rapids. They prefer to come back to the safety of the creek rather than hang on for open water. That's where a life jacket would come in handy, because it gives us confidence that even if we end up in the water we'll be okay and that we can cope with anything.

The life jacket is about getting into a resourceful and confident state, where we know we can cope with whatever life throws at us.

## Mission

Once we're ready to start thinking about leaving the creek we need to understand what our mission is. It's only once we know our mission that we can look at a map and understand the routes that will best enable us to accomplish it.

It's no use just grabbing the paddle and getting the hell out of the creek. Without a mission how will we know what direction to take at the first fork? How will we know it's not another creek?

All the heroes on the TV seem to have a mission to save the world from the bad guys. We therefore know when they meet a bad guy that they're going to take action. There's no doubt in your mind because that's their mission. That's what our mission is about – knowing what we stand for and what we will take action to move towards. It's only once we know this that we can move on to looking at who else might want to journey with us.

## Guides and Travellers

Once we understand our mission it's important that we find people who are going to be able to help us. We might be able to get out of the creek on our own but we stand a better chance if we find people to guide us, and others we can travel with – realizing that not everyone who is a good guide would make a great companion and fellow traveller, and vice versa.

This step in the process is as much about our relationship with our network as it is building the network. We can have thousands of people in our network, but if they don't like or trust us, or us them, what's the point?

The Guides and Travellers step is about identifying your potential network. It's also about developing relationships with those who boost our energy, and minimizing time spent with those who drain our energy.

## Map

When we're up the creek it's not always easy to understand the routes out of it, especially when the tall creek walls are surrounding us. It's easy to think there are no routes out, and believe ourselves to be stuck.

Plotting a map with all the possible routes out helps expand our thinking, and helps us understand all the possibilities that exist. In the long term we'd like to understand the routes that will help us achieve our mission. In the short term we may just need to understand how to get out of the creek.

## Compass

When walking, even if we've got a map, we can use a compass to plot the course and help us understand where we are in relation to the map, and to our intended destination.

We have our own inner compass, an inner wisdom – some would say intuition. Once we've worked out all the possible routes out of the creek it's our inner compass, our intuition, that will determine which direction we take.

This step is also about being authentic and true to ourselves – following our own true north.

## Paddle

Once we've undertaken the other steps there is only one way out of the creek, and that is to find our paddle (or other means of momentum) and use it. To take personal responsibility for the necessary action and to take the first and subsequent steps.

You may find that different metaphorical steps to these come to mind. Listen to that inner knowing, and amend my suggestions until you've got a clear and detailed action plan that feels just right. One that will enable you to go with the flow and stay on track.

If you haven't already done this, you can then translate the action plan and apply it to the situation in hand. For example, what does stopping mean in reality, and what about finding guides and travellers? What do you need to do, who needs to know about it and when will you take the first step?

Once out of the creek you may find it very easy to go with the flow and to stay on track.

Sometimes, however, we find other obstacles that hinder our progress. The next chapter considers times when you're feeling like a fish out of water, and helps you to understand what steps to take to once again be swimming towards your goal.

# CHAPTER 9

# LIKE A FISH OUT OF WATER

"I am feeling like a fish out of water," said Alice before she headed off for an interview for a role she'd wanted for some time.

As I'm sure has happened numerous times in offices up and down the land – and around the globe and back – Alice's statement generated a number of responses from her colleagues – along the lines of:

"You'll be okay once you get going."

"After the first few minutes you'll have forgotten your nervousness, and be remembering why you want the job."

"You just need to expand/step out of/blow up your comfort zone."

"You'll be fine."

And so on.

Which is generally, in my experience, met not by "Oh yes, of course you're right, silly of me not to notice," but by increasing panic!

Until I wrote this chapter, and started applying the insights to coaching clients, I had certainly been one of those telling people, in response to "I'm feeling like a fish out of water" statements, that they'd soon get over their nerves and be perfectly fine.

What I now realize is why these words are the wrong advice to be giving.

But I'm getting ahead of myself – which is what feeling like a fish out of water is all about.

This chapter will help you view the fish and the water, and to understand how to move around the landscape differently. If the saying doesn't currently resonate, to enable you to get the most from the chapter, think of any situation you're stuck about and which you might be able to apply the saying to.

How satisfied do you feel with the current situation on a scale of 0–10?

Now please put the situation you're wanting insight on to the back of your mind.

There are a few sayings where my suggestion before reading the chapter is to go back to before you were stuck, i.e., in this case, go back into the water and answer the questions imagining what it will be like to be out of the water.

The reason for this is that feeling like a fish out of water is very stressful, and I imagine there might be some fear around it. After all, a fish isn't going to last that long out of the water!

The problem with trying to find solutions when we're stressed is we don't really have access to the part of our brain that will be able to easily and effortlessly find a solution. We need therefore to find a means of reducing the fear, and accessing the creative part of our brain – in other words, to go back in time to before we were stressed.

Which means you need to do whatever makes most sense for you to imagine you're safely swimming in water, and reflect on the following questions – remembering there is no odd or weird, just what comes to mind while you allow your unconscious to do the hard work for you while you have some fun playing with the metaphor:

- What sort of fish are you – species, size, shape, colour?
- What water are you in – size, colour, temperature, visibility?
- What water are you headed for – size, colour, temperature?
- What's between the two sets of water – path, height, any obstacles?
- Can the water be made bigger?
- Can you make the two sets of water nearer to each other?
- Were you in or out of the water – i.e., was it the thought of being out of the water that you felt stuck about, or imagining you were?
- Were you mid-air or on the ground – moving or still?
- What was stopping you going back in the water?
- How far away from the water were you?
- How long had you been out of the water?

- If you took the fish to accident and emergency what would the doctor say its condition really was?
- Would a fisherman agree with the doctor's assessment?

Before going further, reflect on the current real-life situation – how does it feel? Could you already be becoming unstuck, or even be back on track?

Having explored the landscape, you now have a few options:

- Explore the imagined landscape some more.
- Make changes to your imagined fish and water landscape.
- Imagine moving from the current landscape into a new one.
- Play around with the saying and get a little absurd (see Part 3 for more on this – my particular favourite is being a fish out of sparkling water).

You'll notice that, unlike other chapters, the above list doesn't include going out into nature to explore the metaphor in real life. It's not just a landscape but includes a fish. Which means, unlike other sayings where we can physically go into the landscape and explore solutions in real life, being a fish out of water would be very hard to replicate. Being a human in water is the nearest I can think of but, while imagining that might give us some insight, doing it in reality is unlikely to be helpful or safe. This may therefore explain why some of the solutions within this chapter are a little more logical than can be found in other chapters.

Let's explore the saying some more because there are some very interesting insights to be gleaned from doing this.

For once let's visit real life for a moment, and consider the situations you might be using this saying about. It's generally used when we are out of our comfort zone and dealing with the unknown.

In other words, we might be:

- Meeting new people
- Visiting new places
- Learning new skills
- Having new experiences
- Being confronted with new beliefs

By using the saying we are suggesting that this new situation is not something we are feeling very comfortable about – we are seeking insight on how to act, what to say or do in this new environment. There is an awkwardness in the current situation that is stopping us behaving naturally.

The question to answer is how we can stop feeling, looking or sounding like a fish out of water when faced with something new?

While there is the "odd", in every sense, fish that can survive out of water, the saying is used to reflect that the person fears being out of place and feels very uncomfortable, and – while I am not sure it is ever used in this sense – taken to its extreme it could potentially mean death!

A fish out of water is in no-man's-land, on a journey to somewhere else. There is a common image of a goldfish moving from its current bowl into a larger one, in mid-flight between the two. A scary place to be indeed.

Like that fish out of water we imagine slowly suffocating as our ability to get the oxygen we need diminishes. As we imagine that happening, it is easy to understand the panic starting to rise and, if we're not careful, a full-blown panic attack ensuing. The problem with that happening is it further inhibits our ability to make rational decisions about how to get back in the water and back to safety.

There are, therefore, a number of factors to be considered:

- How to stop the panic or feelings of discomfort and allow yourself instead to see the opportunities that exist to get back into water.
- How to determine if something is stopping you going back into water.

- How to understand whether going back into "old" water is the best solution or whether going into "new" water might be better.
- How to find out if someone else can help you.

Remember the comments from Alice's colleagues at the start of this chapter? Comments like:

"Oh, you'll get used to it."

"It's not that scary… honest."

"Time to get out of your comfort zone."

These are unhelpful comments, and further examining the saying "like a fish out of water" will help explain why.

Remember the saying is helping you understand the internal representations you have for the situation. Using this representation will therefore allow you to uncover the solutions to the current situation.

If we think we are a fish then asking us to become anything else will seem, and would in reality be, impossible. Yes, we can adapt to different environments, but the sort of adaptation we would need to change from a fish who needs water to one who is okay out of it would take millennia, not the timescales we are dealing in.

I read a great quote from Mechthild, a Christian mystic, about finding our element – i.e., fish have the water and birds air. I like the idea that the aim has to be for the fish to stay within its given element – the element that allows it to flourish.

Let's consider therefore the different aspects of the landscape. As you do so you may want to consider how and whether each aspect may allow you to take action and/or feel differently about the current situation.

Here's where we do need to venture away from conventional wisdom and assume fish do have a brain with the ability to analyse and remember past events and imagine future events. That said, there are two time slots for stopping the panic:

- In advance of leaving the water
- Once out of the water

Many "new" situations are not thrust upon us without warning (if they are, this set of solutions won't work!) We often have prior knowledge of the new situation and therefore can prepare for it. In many instances, for example, there will be advance warning that you need to leave the current area of water and move to another area.

There are many things we can do when we are still in the current water to prepare for the journey. We could:

- Learn from our past.
- Find out from others who have made the leap.
- Find out why we want to leave the current area of water.
- Find out how long we will really be out of water for.
- Get fitter to enable us to be more effective at moving from A to B (flexibility, agility or any other skills we think would help us to move).
- Practise having time out of the water to enable us to be more comfortable being out of it (we often panic because we don't think we can cope with a situation, even though in fact we can – building confidence will help).
- Move the new water nearer to the current water.

Let's apply these insights to a real-life situation that we might consider ourselves to be "like a fish out of water" in: starting a new job.

1   Find out why you want to come out of the water. Motivation is always a great inspirer of action. If we understand why we need to make the change then we will put up with the "unacceptable" for the time it takes to achieve our goal.

If you are starting a new job, therefore, it is useful to remind yourself of why you have taken it – better prospects, more money, more challenging work, promotion, more responsibilities, better life balance, more of work you like, less of work you don't like, more interesting work?

2    Find out how long you will really be out of water for – you may want to ask about induction programmes, policies, procedures and ways of working so it feels less new more quickly.

3    If you have started new jobs in the past, recall what you did then to make the situation feel more familiar more quickly. Perhaps it is this past experience that is making you nervous because it took a long time and was a painful process in the past – in which case point 4 below might help.

4    Learn from others. Find out how others have made the transition easier for themselves – what worked, what didn't.

5    Move the new water nearer the current water – this is touched on above in that it is about reducing the amount of time out of water. However, moving it nearer might be about making the journey in smaller steps rather than one big leap.

6    Perhaps think about taking on new responsibilities over a period of time – or think about how you're already using some of the skills. This can help you get to your new water without really noticing; you have been slowly developing your skills over time and have already made a number of small leaps out of water. This new job is simply another step along that path.

7    Practise having time out of water. When I first started my NLP Practitioner course, we were asked to do something different every day. Examples included:

- Taking a different route home
- Brushing our teeth with the opposite hand
- Putting our socks on first
- Eating breakfast before showering
- Eating lunch outside instead of at our desk.

While many routines evolve out of finding effective behaviours and sticking with them, routine can also make us very resistant to trying something new. Just this simple exercise can strengthen the "doing new things" muscle, which in turn reduces panic in these situations.

A few years ago I took a 28-day challenge and did something different every day. I can't recommend enough trying this as a means of getting yourself out of patterns that are keeping you stuck.

8  Preparing for the journey. If you know you are starting a new job then there are lots of things you can do that can help you be more prepared and able to cope with the transition and reduce the fear of newness.

9  Find out about where you will be working – parking, traffic, route, location of places to eat. You may even want to test out your route to work so you are confident about where you are going.

10 You are going to need energy and concentration in the first few weeks as every piece of information coming at you is new; it is useful to consider what you can do to support having that energy and level of concentration available to you. This may include:

- Getting enough sleep in the weeks leading up to the move
- Eating well
- Taking supplements
- Reducing stress in other areas of your life
- Doing things you enjoy doing
- Not having as busy a social life
- Doing things you know relax and rejuvenate you
- Drinking enough water
- Exercise

11 Find out about the people you will be working with. LinkedIn can be a very useful source of information.

12 Refresh yourself on the new skills you will be using – books, YouTube, Ted Talks, course notes – anything to increase your confidence level and make it less daunting.

How might you be able to apply the tactics above in order to feel less like a fish out of water when you finally do leave the water?

This list is not exhaustive – you may therefore want to consider how you personally relate to the saying.

Have you already taken the leap? Are you stuck somewhere? Are you just nervous? In other words, what are the exact reasons that lie behind your use of the saying?

When you are using the saying today in this example what does it mean?

Using a graphic might help you understand more about your internal representation, and therefore provide more insight on how to resolve it. Especially if you use the exploration of the saying here as a guide to expand your ways of thinking about the situation.

You may already have noticed that you are thinking about the new situation differently. That you are feeling less like a fish out of water, and more like your normal self.

The solutions thus far have tackled reducing the likelihood of panic ahead of the "journey". This assumes some advance warning of either the journey or the fact that you will react to it like a fish out of water. This foresight is not always available and sometimes we suddenly find ourselves like a fish out of water unexpectedly, with no prior warning.

There are plenty of things that can be done in this situation, the aim being to reduce panic and not further exacerbate the situation.

There are three areas help can come from, as illustrated on the following page:

## Body

Panic even for a fish will have an impact on the physical body. A tense body has a number of drawbacks – in the case of the fish, perhaps tension will prevent it from being able to get back in the water.

For us humans a tense body will close down access to our creative mind.

The aim must be to find ways to relax the body and to allow that relaxation to filter through to our thinking and feeling.

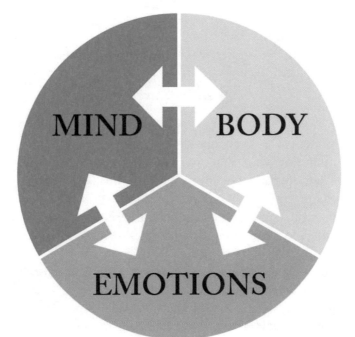

## Mind

Much of feeling like we are a fish out of water is in fact thinking like a fish out of water – we find ourselves out of water and relative safety and panic and start to tell ourselves:

"I've never done this before."
"I don't know what to do."
"This is going to be hard."
"I can't do this."
"This is impossible."
"I'll die."

Unfortunately, what we tell ourselves will impact how we act.

The key is in noticing the language your internal chatter is using, and ensuring that it's supporting the outcome you want. Which means you need to change the language as soon as you notice it is hindering your progress.

Language it would be useful to be hearing could include:
"I can do it."

"How exciting!"

"How easy will that be?!"

A more positive mindset will allow for a more relaxed body and positive emotions.

## Emotions

Emotions are harder to change as they're often the outcome of what we're thinking or what we're doing with our body. However, as the diagram demonstrates, changing our emotions can also have an impact on our mind and body.

Reducing the panic or replacing it with excitement or some other helpful emotion such as confidence or positivity will help you no longer feel like a fish out of water.

Confidence, for example, can often be achieved by recalling and reliving every moment of a time when you've experienced confidence; by seeing what you saw then, hearing what you heard and feeling what you felt. You can even take on the same body posture and tonality.

Likewise, positivity can be achieved by applying our own prescription of activities that help us achieve a more positive state of mind. Here's my prescription that I go to when in need of a little more positivity:

- Doing more things that bring me joy and doing less of the things that don't.
- Doing things that make me laugh.
- Steering well clear of the miserable mackerels in my life.
- Looking for the best in others.
- Stopping, looking, listening and taking time out.
- Remembering we get what we focus on.
- Ensuring I believe "I can do it".
- Noticing the language I'm using and impact that it might be having.
- Exploring the impact the food I'm eating is having on my well-being.
- Moving the body – it never fails to amaze me how just going for a walk can shift my mood.

- Getting enough sleep.
- Drinking enough water.
- And listening to music that makes my heart sing.

The following is an example of how we really need to be playful and open and not constrain our thinking when initially exploring a landscape.

When first writing this chapter I had a very clear vision of the goldfish jumping between two bowls of water, and the rest of the chapter was written from that perspective. Last night, just as I was falling asleep, an additional idea came to mind, one many of you may have already thought of.

The water level may have dropped, leaving the fish stranded.

Which could lead to a different exploration and different solutions. Who knows, just knowing the tide will be returning in a few hours might change how you're feeling. Alternatively, you may realize that you can move your scaly body enough to get back into the water.

This is a great reminder that staying open to alternative perspectives is essential.

Hopefully this exploration has helped you understand how you might be able to make changes to the current picture that represents being like a fish out of water. As you make these changes notice how either you're no longer a fish, or the fish does end up happily back in the water.

Once you're happily swimming in the river, or other expanse of water, you may find it very easy to go with the flow and keep yourself headed towards your destination. In which case keep doing what you're doing.

Or you might feel as if you just want to stay where you are, and bury your head in the sand. The next chapter helps you to explore that metaphorical landscape to enable you to take your head out of that sand and head towards your goal.

# CHAPTER 10

# HEAD IN THE SAND

One solution suggested in every chapter (except the "fish out of water" chapter) is to go to the landscape and enact the saying. I promise you don't have to go and follow my lead with this one – unless you want to try it.

I hadn't intended to take this picture, but I came across a lovely big hole on my local beach and decided it was too good an opportunity to miss. Imagine the surprise of the guy walking his dog who was asked by someone he had never met to take a picture, and then watched as I posed for it by putting my head in the sand!

I can remember looking back to being married and describing myself as having been happy as a pig in muck! I thought that was how relationships were supposed to be – I didn't question what love was; I didn't question the feelings of jealousy, attachment and neediness. It was only later, once the relationship failed, that I realized I had short-changed myself – I had short-changed us. I hadn't thought about what I wanted. My head would have remained firmly in the sand, oblivious to the happiness I was hiding from, if my then-husband hadn't shaken me out of my trance. I think that's a great word to use to describe it – we're in a trance, unable to see that we're not living an authentic and happy life. It's like living with a thin veil between us and life.

This is a hard saying to relate to because it's not generally one we'd use to describe a situation. After all, I'm not sure that we can ever think of ourselves as having our head in the sand. I certainly didn't and yet it was obvious to everyone around me. I believed the excuses I was giving about why my life was like it was, about why we were where we were and why I hadn't taken the appropriate action.

With the other sayings in this book, we acknowledge that we'd like to move forward but something is stopping us. When we have our head in the sand, by contrast, we don't think we need to be anywhere other than where we are. We're happy with just getting by – we don't know that life could be any different than it is and we think this is it; or we blame everyone else for our current situation.

So, if you're reading this and acknowledging that you've got your head in the sand then I commend you!

Even if you don't think you've got *your head in the sand have* a read anyway – you might be surprised.

What I need to do here is describe some of the patterns of this behaviour in real life before we go metaphorical. I'm convinced that if you can't relate to this metaphor it won't work its magic – it can't. If you can't see how you might have your head in the sand then the solutions won't work either. In the same way as you listen to someone giving you directions to their house, think you know the way, and then get lost mid-route and wish you'd paid more attention.

We only pay attention if we think it relates to us and our situation, and since most of us like to think we're taking personal responsibility for and have personal control over our lives, we'll often deny our head is anywhere near the sand.

The content of this chapter is therefore a little different, in that the beginning is about helping you discover in what way you might have your head in the sand. There's also a section towards the end about helping a person who has someone else in their life who has their head in the sand.

If you already recognize that you have your head in the sand, you can skip this next section and get on with working on how to get your head out. If you're wondering if you have your head in the sand, or perhaps believe you definitely don't have (and are just reading this out of curiosity), then consider whether any of the following situations are true for you.

## Recurring Patterns

We so often get caught up in the content of a situation – x said this, and then y did that, and then I said this, etc. – and forget that often when we're stuck there's a pattern to the stuckness. Such as:

- My boss is a bully (and this is my fifth bullying boss).
- My partner has been unfaithful (and this is my fourth unfaithful partner).
- The dance teacher doesn't understand how to motivate me (and this is the 15th dance teacher who has failed to motivate me).
- The diet doesn't work (and this is the 35th diet that hasn't worked).
- Clients just don't get what we're about (and this is the 50th client who's rejected me).
- You made me angry (and you're the 15th person to make me angry this month).

The common denominator here is you – and what you need to take your head out of the sand to understand is that you're the one who has:

- allowed the last five bosses to bully you by not taking the appropriate action;
- acted as if being unfaithful in your last four relationships was acceptable;
- been unmotivated in the last 15 dance classes;
- tried 35 diets that didn't work;
- approached 50 clients, and got zero sales from them;
- allowed another person's actions to make you angry.

One clue to whether you're stuck in this pattern is if you reacted angrily to any of these statements; if you said, for example:

- "But that boss was a bully – it isn't my fault – don't make me out to be the one to blame."
- "But my partner was the one who was unfaithful – what could I do about it – I loved them and they told me they loved me, and I believed them."
- "But anyone would get angry if someone did that to them."

I am not condoning bullying, unfaithful partners or any unacceptable behaviour. I repeat, I am NOT condoning the other person's behaviour – they certainly have their own problems to sort out. But so do we all – and burying our head and blaming other people won't sort our problems out.

Bullies are bullies because they see weakness in another – have you ever seen anyone successfully bully a strong, confident person? No, because bullies generally get their own self-esteem by feeling that they can exert power over another person. If they can't do that, their desire to bully diminishes. Which means burying our head in the sand is about avoiding dealing with our own self-confidence or feelings of self-worth and possibly assertiveness. (Please note these are examples only, and there are numerous other reasons why we might not change our behaviour when faced with bullying – the head-in-sand aspect is that we're not changing our behaviour to deal with it.)

While a few people are completely surprised when faced with infidelity, the majority, after the event, are not – "I shouldn't have been in the relationship to start with," "I knew something was wrong," "we didn't communicate", and so on. Which means that by burying our head in the sand, we're avoiding dealing with why we don't listen to our intuition, or set boundaries with others, or communicate our feelings to them.

Anger is an interesting emotion, and when we're in its thrall it's very hard to understand that it's us who has chosen to be angry about the situation, and not the situation that has made us angry. I'd also suggest there are times when anger is a very healthy emotion to play. The clue was in the statement "the 15th person this month you got angry with". Which means we're avoiding dealing with our anger-management issues – by burying our head in the sand.

If you're still vehemently denying any wrongdoing, perhaps that's the mountain you need to get over – a belief in right or wrong, or belief that less than positive feedback makes you somehow a lesser person. I was discussing mental health with someone, and was interested to learn that there are a number of continuums that mental health can be measured on:

- Negative mental health to positive mental health
- Bad mental health to good mental health
- Unhealthy mental health to healthy mental health

I personally find use of the pairs "negative/positive" or "bad/good" to be unhelpful because they feel like very judgemental descriptions. "Unhealthy and healthy" provides a better description, and it's easier to explore where we are on the continuum without beating ourselves up. Much better to see your anger as an unhealthy behaviour rather than negative, bad or wrong!

Which means that you're not wrong, and it's not negative or a bad thing to have another bullying boss, or be angry at the 15th person this month, it's just unhealthy. Taking your head out of the sand will help you acknowledge that, and also help you identify healthy behaviours to replace the current behaviours. How else will you avoid bullies and unfaithful partners, or lose weight? After all, currently it's your head in the sand that is resulting in you not having the job, relationship or body of your dreams!

Once you've recognized you've got your head in the sand, you may well take it out – and instantly realize that one of the other sayings now relates to you. You want a loving relationship and therefore realize you feel like a fish out of water around potential loving partners, which is why you've ended up with prats in the past, because at some level they didn't threaten your own low belief about yourself. In which case, why not take that situation to the chapter on that saying?

If you've got this far, and now acknowledge you have your head in the sand but are resisting and just not sure how to change this, then read on. Just like feeling like a fish out of water, this saying does have the potential to come with stress and fear. A fear that may be the very reason you're keeping your head in the sand – you may believe that there will be less stress and fear if you keep your head down.

If that's the case, you may want to read Chapter 4 for common reactions to the process to help you deal with the fear before answering some of the questions here. Unless of course you can park your fear for the moment as we explore the saying – there's certainly more chance of being able to do that if we use the metaphor than if we were to discuss the real-life situation. See what feels workable for you – this book isn't about dragging you out of your comfort zone kicking and screaming.

How satisfied do you feel with the current situation – on a scale of 0–10?

Now please put the situation you're wanting insight on to the back of your mind.

Imagine your head is really, literally in the sand and answer the following questions:

- Describe the setting – location, time of year, time of day, temperature
- Describe the sand – colour, temperature, size of grains, how much there is (depth, expanse)
- Can you see anything else other than sand?
- How deep is your head in the sand?
- Is any more of your body in the sand?
- What's stopping you taking your head out of the sand?
- What happens if you imagine taking your head out of the sand?
- How are you breathing?
- Can you stand up?
- What can you hear?
- Can you make your body more comfortable?
- What clothes are you wearing?
- Is there any water nearby?
- Perhaps a strange idea, but if you're still struggling to shift perspective, and since sand gets everywhere, what about envisaging getting sand into your socks or underwear!? Sometimes we're just too comfortable in a situation; envisaging and feeling sand on your skin, irritating you, may just provide the motivation to move that you needed.

Before going on, reflect on the current real-life situation – how does it feel? You may already have taken your head out of the sand. As I type that, I realize that to even be able to answer many of the questions you probably need to have taken your head out of the sand already. How does it feel to realize you have had to do that? What needs to happen to stop you putting your head back in the sand?

Of all the chapters in this book, I do think this saying is the hardest to shift metaphorically – not impossible, just the hardest. Mainly because as soon as we've got our head out of the sand, we're faced with the reason why we put it there in the first place. We may have put our head in the sand because we were scared, or didn't know what to do. When we take our head out of the sand therefore, those circumstances will still be there and we still have work to do on the situation. Hopefully one of the other sayings will then resonate.

As I said earlier in the chapter, others can see what we're doing more easily than we can. If you're reading this hoping to find clues on how to coach someone who has their head buried in the sand, then read on.

After coaching others for nearly 20 years I realize that those who coaching worked for were those who:

- had identified something they wanted in life;
- were motivated to have the new outcome;
- were motivated to take the necessary action to change;
- were stuck and knew it;
- wanted help to get there.

Like anyone addicted to certain behaviours (whether alcohol, social media, anger, chocolate or running away), a person with their head in the sand has to want to release the addiction.

Until they acknowledge their addiction, they will continue to be in the thrall of the behaviour or substance.

We can tell others what to do till we're blue in the face; however, unless they truly understand the reasons for changing, why would they?

Coaching can be very frustrating – I might be able to see what's going on much sooner than my client, but telling them won't help them, and as I could be wrong anyway that may even make things worse.

Forcing coaching is a bit like picking someone up at Everest base camp and just dropping them at the summit. They won't be acclimatised to the environment and could well die. We all need to go on a journey of discovery, and trying to take short cuts isn't effective for long-term change. When a cat moves to a new house it requires a few weeks before it gets used to its new surroundings. Then when it does venture out, it does so very cautiously, always ensuring there's a free path from where it is back into the space it now feels safe in. This is how to approach coaching.

All you can do is leave the door open, to allow them to pop their head out of the sand now and again and realize it is safe to do so.

The most effective way of motivating anyone out of the hole is using their values – i.e., the pain they want to move away from and the pleasure they want to move towards.

Look out for statements that demonstrate a motivation for an outcome, and see if you can link the head in the sand activity to it. For example, they may express a desire for a long-haul holiday, but say they don't have the money. You could point out they could earn more money if they left this job (and the bullying boss!) Or they may express a desire to have more friends – you could point out that uncovering why they keep falling out with people would help.

One word of caution. You can't change anyone, and I'd certainly ask you to look within yourself to understand why you're wanting someone else to take their head of the sand, i.e., what will you get as a result of this? If it's something purely selfish, then you may want to explore how to let this need to change another person go (perhaps one of the sayings in the book describes how you feel).

If you're affected by the current behaviour of the other person because they're your mother, father, child, other relative, partner, friend, colleague, boss… then you could:

- Tell them what you'll do if they can't change – i.e., if this isn't resolved I'm leaving.
- Remind them of the repercussions of their behaviour, especially when it's counter to their stated outcome – you won't have pain-free knees if you carry that weight.
- Highlight the conflicting beliefs they're operating.
- Call them on their behaviour – i.e., hold a mirror up to their repeating patterns.

Just be careful – of course we can encourage and support them on their journey, but they have to go on it for themselves. You also have to look after your own well-being; you can't spend all of your time and energy trying to change another person. After all, sometimes that might be all they need – to see you modelling what you've been encouraging them to do. Remember, sometimes we see a "fault" in another because we can't see it in ourselves.

One off-the-wall suggestion: when we want others to change we can become quite fixated on it happening, and this can come out in the words, tone and actions we use. Sometimes it's these very behaviours that the other person resists – "No one is going to tell me what to do – I'm going to keep my head in the sand if it kills me – at least this is something I chose to do!" There's a great technique called perceptual positions that requires imagining standing in their shoes. It might help take the pushy or controlling energy out of your words and behaviours and therefore tone down the negative energy the other person is feeling from you. You'll find more about this process on my website and LinkedIn page.

Of course, this process can be used in many situations, not just when dealing with someone with their head in the sand.

One final exercise you might like to try if you're still feeling as if you've got your head in the sand is to follow the process outlined in previous chapters and describe the landscape.

For example, if I imagine my head being in the sand I think of a desert. Which means when I pull my head out of the sand all I'm going to see is more and more sand. Nothing but sand that stretches on to the horizon – oh, and uncomfortable heat!

I can certainly see why we can find it hard to see the opportunities that exist within this situation and landscape.

Once we understand the internal picture we have of an issue, it's time to play with the representation and see what happens as we do this:

- I could imagine my head in a sandpit that is surrounded by children laughing and playing creative games. I can then imagine joining in with them for a while and noticing what solutions appear.

- My head could be in sand adjacent to an oasis and all I need to do is walk to it and take a cool, long drink of water and sit in the shade for a while.
- Or I could be on my local beach and just need to walk away – NOW!

I know this might all sound weird, but it's really no weirder than what we're doing when we describe ourselves as "burying our head in the sand." It's not a reality, but it is impacting how we're thinking and therefore behaving. The exploration here is simply providing the brain with a few more options to consider. One of which might open the connection within your brain to the solution to the current situation. After all we do know what to do – we're just allowing fear to feed the resistance to not knowing.

Other options to re-look at the internal representation include:

- Getting out your mobile and calling international rescue, and being flown to another landscape.
- Taking your head out of the sand and realizing you're surrounded by other, expert explorers, and they and you have all the necessary equipment to get out of there.
- Waking from a dream, realizing that you've already got all the resources you need in the current situation and it was simply a nightmare, and it is now time to start living a different dream in reality.

Next time you think you might be burying your head in the sand, remember – it may be all plain sailing from here!

Once you've got your head out of the sand you may need to reflect on all the sayings again (see the index) to see which one best fits how you're now feeling. Unless of course you're already back on track and headed for your desired destination.

The next chapter looks at what options you have if you're describing your situation as being like you're out on a limb or in at the deep end.

# OUT ON A LIMB/IN AT THE DEEP END

These aren't sayings I often get chance to explore in a real landscape. They do however lend themselves very nicely to the use of collage.

At a personal development workshop I attended, the course leader spoke about swimming in a swimming pool, and then having the sides of the pool pulled away and realizing that you were swimming in the ocean.

That description had a very profound impact on me, and felt very much like being thrown in at the deep end. Yet at the same time, I could feel that the boredom of swimming in a pool helped release any lingering desire to hold on to what was comfortable.

At the end of the workshop we spent some time making collages, to represent insights gained from the workshop, but also for future use in coaching – for both ourselves and our clients.

See the collage card I made to represent swimming in the ocean beyond the swimming pool on page 141.

What additional guidance comes to mind as you view this image? Perhaps consider what the card would say to you if it had a voice.

Today as I write, my attention is drawn to the swimmer with breathing apparatus – a reminder perhaps that the scary feeling when the pool's sides were taken away was only because the water was so, perhaps too, deep. Perhaps I therefore added the breathing apparatus to help to reduce my fear at the thought of being there?

Looking at this image is a lot like constructing and imagining our landscapes – each time, we pay attention to a different aspect of the

landscape. Today I noticed the breathing apparatus, another time I noticed the turtle. Each a clue in its own right, that our unconscious is able to make sense of the landscape and apply the insight gained to our current situation.

Unlike in most of the other chapters in this book, here I'm covering two sayings, not one. The reasons are that I couldn't decide which resonated the most, and they have a very similar energy. An energy of needing to release the barriers to forward progress.

## Out on a Limb

Out on a limb is an interesting saying, not least because many people don't even associate it with trees. In this context, we're definitely using it to describe going out on a limb of a tree, to the very edge where it's much thinner and much more likely to break.

If you resonate with this saying, or can relate it to the situation you're stuck about, consider your answer to the following questions:

- Describe the limb – size, shape, width, length, sturdiness, height above ground level.
- What is the limb attached to?
- Does it feel precarious, and if so why?
- Are you standing on the limb, sitting, hanging from it, crawling or something else?
- How long is the limb?
- How far have you already travelled along it?
- How far is there to go till the end, till it breaks or it is no longer able to hold your weight?
- How big is the drop?
- What's below you – I think this, particularly considered together with "How big is the drop?", is an especially important question that will highlight why we're stuck, and why we're unable to move forward.
- Are you able to move?
- What happens if you move forward?
- Can you go back the way you came – back along the limb and then perhaps into the tree?

As you may have found from previous chapters, sometimes just answering questions about the current situation somehow shifts the situation. It's as if understanding more about the current situation helps a solution to appear.

If you've already noticed that has happened, then you may want to write an action plan about what you're going to do, and when.

If it would be helpful to explore this saying more deeply, your options are the same as for the other sayings:

- Explore the imagined landscape some more – draw it, for instance, do a collage or a map – the aim being to know and understand it more fully so that solutions and alternatives are more obvious.
- Go and visit a real-life tree limb – perhaps this is not as helpful as for some of the other sayings; and remember that the aim is certainly to stay safe!
- Make changes to your imagined tree/limb situation.
- Imagine moving from the current landscape into a new one.
- Play around with the saying and get a little absurd with it (see Part 3 where you may be invited to consider being out on a rut or can't see the tree for the limb!)

I recently visited the Birnam Oak, a tree over 500 years old that inspired Shakespeare. Some of its larger branches now have support to stop them from breaking. The Birnam Oak reminds us to explore ways of making the limb we're out on more secure – fattening it, providing support, bringing the ground or river below nearer to the limb so it's not so far to fall.

I love the diversity of the sayings used in the book, because while they all use landscapes they're all subtly different in what they're suggesting happened before, what's happening now and what might happen in the future.

For example, before we'd describe ourselves as being "out on a limb" wouldn't we just be "on a limb"?

Which seems to suggest that, while we might want to just make changes to the constructed image we have for "out on a limb", we're still going to be on the limb, and for a majority of people the aim must be to get away from the tree altogether. Otherwise any changes to being on a limb are only temporary – sooner or later we need to be leaving the limb, and moving into a new landscape.

Making changes to the current image will definitely help if there's any negative emotion connected with feeling like you're out on a limb.

Many people when using this saying find that it's the feelings associated with being 'out on a limb' that keep them stuck. It's the feelings that freeze them in the current situation. (Although if you resonate with my use of the word freeze you may just want to imagine thawing the situation in order to be able to move – just a thought.) It might therefore be important and useful to make changes first to allow the emotion – which is fear in many instances – to reduce enough for you to be able to consider moving, thus enabling you to notice and consider a wider range of solutions.

For me "out on a limb" suggests that we've already passed a point of no return. If you could turn back, you'd have done so when you were just "on a limb". Out on a limb suggests that you can't go back – only forward. The challenge then is to determine how to make forward motion easier, and to let go of and get out of the current stuck state.

Which leads to you the following questions and, once you have your answers, to imagining making the necessary changes to the image you have:

1   What options are there for the future?
   • Move back – most unlikely but see if it's possible.
   • Move further along the limb till it breaks.
   • Jump
   • Fall
   • Fly
   • Float
   • Swing
   • Step off
   • Parachute

- Paraglide
- Slide
- Zip wire

2   Are there any other options I've missed from the list?

3   What's stopping you from taking one of these actions?

4   What are you most afraid of – the height, the limb breaking, falling, hurting yourself – I'd suggest the answer might provide a clue about what to do to reduce the fear.

5   What would make you feel safer and/or reduce the fear?
   - Harness, or something that breaks your fall or stops it altogether.
   - Softer landing – water, bubblewrap, leaves, hay, mud, sea, trampoline!
   - Less of a drop to ground level (either move the ground up, or the limb down).
   - Making you lighter.

Imagine making the changes that came to mind as you answered those questions. Keep going until you're able to get off the limb (in whatever way makes most sense to you), and move forward away from this landscape towards your desired outcome.

This phrase is also a little like feeling like a fish out of water, in that there is a possibility we knew we were going to feel like we were out on a limb even before we took that first step along the limb.

Before we take a step onto the limb, therefore, there are things we could do:

- Check the strength of the limb.
- Choose a sturdier limb.
- Practise balancing on a limb.
- Reduce our fear of heights.
- Find a different route to our destination – i.e., not climb the tree in the first place, or climb down it and then decide how to get where we're going.
- Do a risk assessment, and determine how real our fears are.

The aim is to make changes to the constructed image and as a result feel better, and more able to take the necessary action(s) in the real-life situation.

As you made these changes and explored the landscape, what did you notice? Sometimes the changes are so subtle they're outside our awareness, and it's only when we start taking action that we realize something shifted.

Consider the original situation – how satisfied do you feel about it now? What action will you take today to start to get back on track?

In this chapter, alongside "out on a limb", I'd also like to look at "in at the deep end". This is perhaps what happens when we let go of the limb – i.e., we don't actually reduce our fear, just move further into a still very scary landscape.

## In at the Deep End

Should "in at the deep end" be a better saying to describe your current situation, then consider your answer to the following questions about the image you've constructed that represents this saying.

- Describe the end – where, what, how big, colours, textures, surroundings.
- What's the weather like, and what about the weather forecast?
- Describe what's deep about it.
- What's at the opposite end?
- Where's at the shallow end?
- What's above you?
- What's below the deep end?
- Where are the exits?
- How long have you been in the deep end?
- How did you get into the deep end – swam there? thrown? walked? jumped? woke up?
- What's stopping you from getting out of the deep end?
- Are you able to swim or float around the landscape?
- Are you on your own?
- Would any equipment help – breathing apparatus? floating aids?

- What happens if you change the deep end – such as from the swimming pool to the sea, as in my example.

What other aspects of the deep end have the above questions not uncovered? Explore those aspects by answering your own questions as they help you more fully understand the landscape you've constructed.

The aim is to understand the current landscape, and then to make changes. Changes that involve either changing the current landscape itself, or moving to another landscape.

In at the deep end also reminds me of up the creek without a paddle, because the first action has to be to make yourself safe; then once you're safe you can more practically determine the best course of action out.

How can you feel safe in the current situation?

From this feeling safe point of view, what actions do you need to take to get out of the deep end? It may be that, feeling safe, you can revisit the questions above as you explore options for getting back on track.

Sometimes, however, it might be being in at the *shallow* end that is the problem!

I hate walking into the sea gradually, inch by inch, immersing my body into the sea. Much better for me to get into water via a ladder straight into its depths. Knowing this is how I feel about swimming in water means I'm not likely to ever worry about being in at the deep end but instead am more likely to hate being at the shallow end.

I'd certainly invite you to play around with this, and any of the sayings, if they don't make sense to you.

Once back on track we might find that we can happily go with the flow – or, less positively, we might start to tread water or go round in circles. If that's the case then the next chapter will help you explore these metaphorical landscapes.

CHAPTER 12

# TREADING WATER/GOING ROUND IN CIRCLES

Have you ever noticed we often think we've solved a problem, but some while later we find ourselves stuck again? Progress has been made, but we've still not achieved our desired outcome. It's as if being stuck has a magnetic hold over us, and thus far we've not managed to break free of its powerful hold to get back on track. That's what going round in circles is like.

When I took David, who resonated with this saying, into a wood the circles he was walking in weren't quite circular for some reason (we never found out why). When I asked him which direction he wanted to go in he was very clear which path he wanted to take. I therefore asked him to start walking in that direction, and to notice what he noticed as he did so. After a few metres he turned round and said: "But I don't want to leave you all behind."

He was with six others on a LYL workshop, using the real landscape to explore the challenges they were all facing, using the process outlined in this book.

After realizing he didn't want to leave us all behind, David came back to walking in his circle in the middle of the wood near to the group. A few minutes later he spied what we all thought was a bridge at the end of a path, in the opposite direction, and asked if we could go that way.

This was a great example of how easily we distract ourselves – like magpies with shiny objects, losing sight of our goal and getting caught up in the tittle-tattle of life. We often do this just in case the other direction might be better, forgetting that half a path never leads anywhere. You have to walk the whole path to get to any destination – even if that particular destination ends up only being a stopping point, a milestone, on the way to another destination.

Continually walking half a path and then changing our mind drains our energy and passion for life. How much better it is to walk a path in its totality, and then to absorb and reflect on the insights when you get to your destination. Once you are there, you can recalibrate and set a new course towards your next destination.

The choice we then have is how long to make each path we walk.

I'd suggest it doesn't matter how long or short the path we walk, as long as we commit to walking the whole of it.

Perhaps that's where so many people go wrong – picking a destination too far away, so that walking the path without distraction is impossible. It's too easy then to end up miles off course – or to walk round in circles, lost!

There are a few different reasons we can find ourselves failing to break free of the circle's hold.

The first reason is that we may simply be stuck again. Isn't that what life is often about: we make progress, we come to a barrier or hurdle of some description, we spend some time getting over, under or round the barrier and then we're off again.

If this is the case, and you've just come to another hurdle, I'd suggest one of the other sayings used in the book might be more appropriate. If so, have a look at the contents page, and check in again about what best describes your current state of stuckness.

Ask yourself: "At this moment in time how would I describe the stuckness?" Not what do you think others would say, or what did you do last time. Today, with this outcome in mind, which saying best describes the current situation? If you discover that another saying describes the situation better, then just pop along to that chapter and notice what you notice as you follow the suggestions there.

Alternatively, treading water, or going round in circles, may very well describe your current stuck state. I've put them in the same chapter because they both describe a state of movement that's not taking us anywhere fast, and yet has an energy of exhaustion, as for example with indecisiveness. It's as if all our energy is being sapped and drained as we simply try to keep our head above water, if that isn't mixing too many metaphors.

If this is your first time treading water or going round in circles, you may want to explore these words in the same way as by undertaking any or all of the following activities:

- Explore the imagined landscape – describe it, draw it, do a collage or a map.
- Physically tread water or walk round in a real circle and find a solution while doing that activity (I accept one may be much easier and safer than the other – please therefore remember to not put yourself in harm's way; although, having just taken up open-water swimming here in Scotland, I may try treading water and noticing what solution appears – I suspect floating may be a less energy-sapping activity).
- Make changes to the image you have of the current water/circle situation.
- Imagine moving from the imagined landscape into a new one.
- Play around with the saying, and get a little absurd – you'll find more about this in Part 3.

What I'd like to explore more is one activity that has been very successful when clients feel like they're going round in circles.

If you're using this saying it's very likely that you have an internal representation for that saying. It might be a vision of the circle or a sense of the circle, or the circle may have or make a sound.

Bring that picture, sound, movement or feeling to mind.

You might not have realized you had an image until I asked the question, but your mind likes to make sense of the language you're using, and will have made sense of it, most likely in the form of a picture, movie, movement or sound.

In one of my workshops Mathias knew what direction (A) he wanted to go in instead of the circle he was currently going round in. He therefore took a pen and drew a line from the original circle towards this destination, A, and noticed what he noticed. He ended up drawing a figure of eight oscillating between A and the original circle. Something he could relate to, having said "Not here again" a few times over the years.

The question I asked Mathias was "What has to happen for you to stop going round in circles?" The answer surprised us both – "Go to destination B".

He then tried drawing round the original circle, following this by drawing a line to B. Mathias was, as we say in the UK, "Happy as Larry", and drew a flower shape with B at its centre, and never went near the original circle.

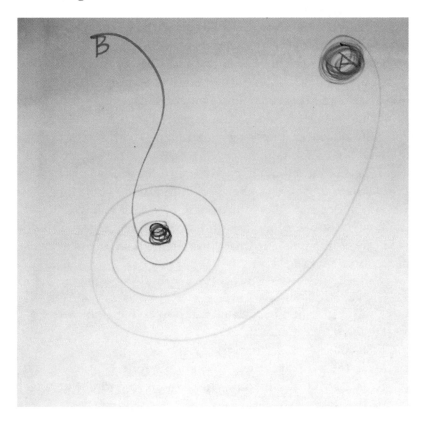

For Louise, a workshop delegate, drawing squares not circles made all the difference!

In none of these instances did we need to understand what this exploration meant or where A or B was. The situation just felt better, and they were more satisfied.

This demonstrated that something had shifted, even if we didn't know (or need to know) what. We then continued the coaching sessions, developing action plans for resolving the situations we'd been talking about.

If sound is more your "thing" you may not find drawing helpful. You want to ask yourself what sound going round in circles has, and how you can change the sound to get to your end destination. Who knows – a song may come to mind, and take you metaphorically on the journey you need to go on to release what's holding you back, and get you back on track.

I've had other clients who need to dance or walk the circle. They walk towards their destination, and then notice what they notice about how to stay at the destination and not migrate back to their circle.

I know it sounds odd, but it's one way our mind is able to make sense of a situation without all the content of day-to-day judgements, musts, oughts and shoulds getting in the way. Thus, we're able to bypass the resistance and barriers to making changes, and therefore are able to find a solution!

Just like David, you can of course do this in reality – take yourself into a landscape of your choosing, start to walk in circles and notice what you notice and follow the questions/prompts above.

With David, lack of a sense of destination seemed to be getting in the way of him breaking free of the circle's hold. If you're like him one solution might be to:

1   Pick a destination.
2   Draw a map and pick a route of how to get from where you are to your destination.
3   Pick your first milestone.
4   Walk the path all the way to that milestone.
5   Reassess your destination, check the map and decide which path to take next.
6   Repeat until there are no more paths to take.

Another means of exploring a saying is to describe it.

When going round in circles the questions might be:

- What are you going round?
- How are you going round?
- Describe the circle – size, shape (NB: it's not always circular even if you're calling it a circle)

- What speed are you going round at? What happens if you slow or quicken the speed?
- What direction do you want to go in?
- What's stopping you going in that direction?

If you're treading water the question might be:

- How are you treading water?
- What water – river, lake, sea, swimming pool, bath?
- What depth of water – are you out of your depth?
- Where's your head in relation to the water?
- What about the time of day or year?
- Describe the water – for example, if it's the sea, waves, current, temperature, wind speed and direction?

The idea is to get a better representation of the landscape. Once you have this perspective it's much easier to be able to plot a route out.

It's worth mentioning again here that if you can't make sense of my questions, you should just think about what questions would make most sense for your landscape. The term "treading water" for me means being in water out of my depth, and treading the water to keep afloat. A client recently interpreted it to mean treading through water – a completely different saying.

It's often about finding the difference that makes the difference. You could change many aspects of the landscape but it wouldn't change how you feel. Then you find the one thing that makes a difference – and everything changes.

For example, with Susan it was the water temperature that made a huge difference. As soon as we warmed up the sea everything changed – she could put her feet on the ground, walk out of the sea, and so on.

In other cases the solution is found by going on an imaginary journey from the current landscape and into another landscape.

Recently Mel thought she might be treading water and/or out on a limb. We discussed which was the more important. I'm sure we'd have got there whichever way round we decided to choose to work on the sayings.

What we did was work on treading water first, and once we'd gone through the process we just checked what had happened to out on a limb.

Mel's journey included her treading water and then getting into a boat, and heading for her dream island. When we checked what had happened to out on a limb, she felt she'd incorporated the feelings associated with this saying in the sense that what those words had conveyed was that she felt as if she was entering uncharted territory. As her antidote included someone on board the boat knowing how to plot a course, the feeling of being out on a limb had subsided, along with her endlessly treading water.

Once Mel felt better, and no longer felt like she was treading water, she was able to identify an action plan associated with the real-life situation, which included finding a mentor to help her as she took her first steps in finding a new job.

You, like Mel, may find that, having explored treading water metaphorically as we have been doing so far in this chapter, something has shifted and you do feel much more confident about moving forward. In which case what's your action plan, who needs to know about it and when will you take the first step?

However, there are times when we keep coming back to the same landscape over and over; either going round in one big circle and not noticing, or swimming for a little while and then starting to tread water again.

I've found as I've been writing the chapters that I've played out the sayings, and as I wrote this chapter I found myself getting very distracted, forgetting what I was supposed to be doing, and doing something else instead. It took every ounce of my willpower to bring myself back to my laptop and keep myself there to finish the chapter.

Isn't that what happens when we're treading water? We know where we want to get to, so we head in that direction but then either get tired, or something else attracts our attention, and we end up still treading water, waiting for something that never comes!!

My own personal experience of treading water, then, isn't about waiting for other people but waiting for me to decide for myself that it's time to push on. The questions I need to ask myself are therefore aligned with what's called the well-formed outcome, a process originating in neuro linguistic programming:

1   Why do I want to get where I'm going?
2   What will it be like when I get there?
3   Can I achieve it alone?
4   How can it dovetail with significant people in my life?
5   When, where and with whom do I want it?
6   What will I lose by leaving where I am?
7   What resources do I need to get there?
8   What's the bigger picture of why this is important?
9   What's the first step?

When going round in circles or treading water it might be any one of these steps that's missing; but the ones that most often trip us up are one, two and six.

Numbers one and two because we need to know where we want to go, and why, in order to put in the effort to leave where we are currently. Treading water might be draining, but so too is swimming the Channel, so I can understand why treading water might be the preferable option.

Number six because we're getting something from the current situation that we don't want to lose. For example, I like my life as it is and a successful published book will certainly change all that; so until I can reconcile myself to that I may very well end up treading water or going round in circles for some time. I need to understand that the peace and solitude I crave, and get currently, can be available to me even as a published author.

As this is a book dealing in metaphors, I'd suggest trying to answer the questions metaphorically first – so, what resources do you need to get from the first landscape to the second? I know it's easier to answer in real life, but you're reading this because you're going round in circles – because you've been here before. Jumping straight back into real life may just mean you miss the nugget that's been hiding from you all along. For example, staying with the round in circles metaphor rather than going back to the real-life situation means any barriers you may have to change in real life are turned down – or it's as if there's a switch and you're keeping it in the off position.

Which means it's perhaps easier to answer the question of what will you lose if you stop treading water or going round in circles –

perhaps it is because as soon as you start swimming you'll go straight into deep water? Remember, in reality we get caught up in the real-life situation and then want to justify why we've not taken the necessary steps out.

More than with any of the other sayings, when we're going round in circles there will be a tendency to go back to where you were before. You may therefore want to find some way of firmly anchoring yourself to the new landscape to stop you being able to go back – remember David thinking about what would keep him on the path he wanted to go along so that he wouldn't get distracted, and wanting to keep near other people. Or, what would keep Mel out of the water and on the island rather than going back into the water?

The answer may require them to make more changes to their landscape – perhaps making the water too hot or too cold to go back into, or having a rope to connect them to the path that stops them going backwards.

The aim is always to embrace the new landscape, as long as it feels better and is more aligned with where you want to be.

Then, and only then, you can go back to the original situation and decide what that means in reality. It might not mean anything other than the change in your feeling about the situation; or it might come with a ready-made action plan, or one you need to develop. Each situation will be different and therefore the solution will be subtly different too. Once we've stopped going round in circles or treading water, we have the option to go with the flow and head towards the ocean, as you will very shortly discover.

There is, however, one more saying that often depicts the final hurdle we may encounter when moving towards a goal in our life, and that's when we hear ourselves saying "I've missed the tide." The next chapter explores the landscape contained within this saying, in order that you may fully be in the flow and headed for the ocean.

# CHAPTER 13

# MISSED THE TIDE

"Missed the tide" is an interesting use of language – and is often used to describe missing that one perfect time to do something, after which there is no other time, ever, when we can undertake the activity. This of course is not true, as the next tide is only ever roughly 12.5 hours away.

But I'm getting ahead of myself, and yet again I feel my behaviour is reflecting what we're often doing when we run the pattern of the saying.

Isn't feeling like we've missed the tide about getting ahead of ourselves? About feeling like we've missed the tide, we're too slow and we need to quicken the pace to keep up with everyone, or we need to take action NOW!!

I'd like to share what happened once when I visited my local beach, as it's a great example of how you don't know what you will discover or notice until you're in nature.

I arrived at Kirkcaldy beach just after low tide, and as I typed time passed and I noticed that the rocks that had been visible had become lost in the sea again – they would be unseen other than by the fish (mackerel at the moment, according to the fishermen) until the next tide.

Timing is everything; we can search for the rocks but those at low tide only become visible for an hour or so every 12.5 hours.

It's useful to understand how this relates to life – patience is often needed before we can see what we need to see. We often judge ourselves or others for not noticing sooner, but judging isn't justified if something is only there to be seen two hours in every 24. Sitting on the beach and just watching at any other time of day, or looking up rather than down the beach, would not have given me that revelation. I had to be there during those two hours facing in that direction to see the uncovered rocks. A great reminder that high or low tide are not the only times of interest when each tide has a duration of 12.5 hours.

I can hear the sea more too, now, as it slowly progresses across the sand to where I'm sitting. Everyone else is further up the beach beyond the high-tide mark, but I needed to write here – and I realize now that this is because this experience had some answers for me regarding this chapter and the one on molehills.

Isn't that useful to know? That if we sit somewhere quietly the tide will come to us? In that context there is no such thing as catching or missing the tide; we need only have patience and to trust it will return.

As with all the sayings, there are a number of different options for exploring the situation you believe – metaphorically – you've missed the tide about:

- Explore the imagined landscape – describe it, draw it, do a collage or a map.
- Actually go to a beach before high or low tide and experience missing it.
- Make changes to the image you have of the tide.
- Imagine moving from the current landscape into a new one.
- Play around with the saying and get a little absurd (you may after all have only missed the wood– see Part 3 for more on this).

Questions to ask yourself as you describe your landscape some more might be:

- "Missed" what about the tide?
- What tide and where?
- If at the ocean, describe the ocean – water, temperature, depth, current, wind, time of day, and so on.

- Where are you in relation to the tide?
- What got in the way of you catching the tide? (Remember to stay metaphorical and not get drawn into the real-life situation).
- What's stopping you from waiting till the next tide?
- When is the next tide?
- What do you need to do to be prepared for the next tide?

The aim is to see the landscape from all perspectives – how would an eagle see the situation? What about a fish? This is about gathering as much data as you can, in order that opportunities can be uncovered and options appear. Even if they're only metaphorical options, a part of you will be able to translate it into real life – but later. For now, stick with the metaphor; it's much easier, and much more likely to uncover what's been keeping you stuck so far.

Missing the tide presupposes that we needed the tide to be at a certain depth to do something, whether that's low tide to uncover the rocks, or high tide to fish, or rising tide to launch a boat.

At all other times, it's simply a self-imposed time we missed – go to any tidal water and look at it, and you'd be hard pushed to notice the difference between now and a few minutes ago. The contours of the beach might mean better waves but, differences caused by a windy or wavy sea aside, look at the tide's edge and it looks the same – water ebbing and flowing.

How do you know that the self-imposed time was the right one – what did you really miss? Stick with the metaphor and imagine the tide that you "missed", and notice what happens in an hour, two hours, four hours, six hours, ten or 11 hours later.

Or, as this is a metaphorical landscape, roll the time back and press "pause" on the movie just before the perfect time; get ready to press "play", and have your second chance again.

Before reading further, try changing aspects of the metaphor, and notice if anything changes about your feelings about the situation, or your understanding of how to resolve what's currently hindering you from moving forward.

- Where is the tide – can you change your relationship to the tide or change the location? You could even imagine chasing the high tide as it moves along the coast.
- Change the time of year or month – this can make it a really low low tide or a really high high tide – or what about a low high tide or high low tide?
- What happens if you change the height of the tide ?
- Does changing your means of transport have an impact – type of boat, means of propulsion (rowing, motor, sail), walking, running, swimming, surfboard, jet ski…?
- Can you imagine going back in time to before you missed the tide?

When we use these sayings sometimes it means we need to find out more about the landscape itself – after all, how much do you know about the tide?

In most places there are two high tides every lunar day, or every 24 hours and 50 minutes, separated by a low tide. The heights of the high and low tides are determined by the position and distance of the moon from Earth. The tide heights are therefore not the same every day, and equinoxes and full moons bring exceptionally high and low tides.

"Missing the tide" is often used to describe a situation where we've missed the optimal time to undertake an activity – but have we? If we explore the non-metaphorical tide for a moment, you'll notice that there is more than just the timing of the high tide to think about.

What depth of tide is needed depends on what you want to do. If you want to play on the beach then a lower tide may be preferable, to allow more sand to be exposed. High tide is better for fishing, and when launching boats the best depth depends on the jetty position.

Here in Burntisland the diving boats tend to leave midway between high and low tide, returning at the same time on the next or subsequent tide. Jet skis are the same, otherwise you're left waiting for the tide to get high enough for them to leave the water via the jetty.

### What height of water is needed to undertake this task?

If you're surfing, then the preferred depth of tide will depend on the location of the tide in relation to the beach, and the angle of slope of the sand into the water. It's the angle that makes the most difference, and is why in some places surfing is better close to the shore, while in others a boat is needed to get you out to the best surfing area.

If you're wanting to go rock-pooling, again it depends on the location of the pools in relation to the high-tide mark.

### What part of the tide is optimal in this situation and set of circumstances?

Weather also plays an important part in tides – it's no use wanting to go fishing, and knowing the sweet spot in the tide for the fish to be swimming past, if it's blowing a hooley and you can't stand up.

Swimming where I live in Scotland is nothing to do with the tide, and all to do with temperature – and you may get to swim comfortably in the water in September, when it's had all summer to warm up!! The water is certainly looking a lot less inviting as I type this, as the cloud has covered the sun and blue water has turned to a grey colour; the wind now feels colder on my skin, too, without the sun adding its warmth.

### How's the weather with you? Is it appropriate to what you wanted to do?

Missing the tide may simply be about waiting for a future tide when the weather is just right.

Wind direction and pressure too – as I sit here the wind has just changed and suddenly the spray (despite an outgoing tide now) is starting to make me wonder if I may need to move. The waves that were very gentle are no longer quite so gentle.

### Has the wind recently changed direction, meaning the optimal time has also changed?

Current also plays a big part when swimming, fishing and sailing. Its strength and direction will alter the impact and effectiveness of an incoming or outgoing tide. It is so easy in some locations to get

carried away by the tide and end up much further down the beach, or even out at sea.

I remember swimming on Whitehaven beach in the Whitsunday Islands in Australia, and being surprised at how far down the beach the tide had taken us despite us thinking we were just swimming back and forth aligned with the rest of the party on the beach.

Swimming wasn't even an option on Daytona beach the day we visited. Even when just paddling we were impacted by the drag of the tide, and the nine-year-old with us had to hold an adult's hand at all times!

*Are you in control of the tide, or are you being dragged along like a piece of jetsam or flotsam? If so, how can you take back control?*

High tide is just one moment – a bit like the gap between an in- and an out-breath. The chances, therefore, of that moment being crucial are very remote – unless of course you're wanting to measure the height of high tide.

There's actually, then, much leeway on what constitutes high tide and therefore any point of the tide you're aiming for. And if you miss this tide, it is absolutely certain that there's another coming in another 12.5 hours' time. If you've missed this opportunity, you just need to consider when the next tide will be.

### Have you constrained the perfect time too much – how much leeway was there? When's the next tide?

Remember, if you're using the saying then there must be another tide. You wouldn't be resonating with the saying if the key component of the saying was missing. If it was a one-off, never-to-be-repeated opportunity, you would not have chosen this saying. If your answer therefore was "I've missed my only opportunity"– think again.

The other thing to know about tides is they're not the same height every day. I'm currently sitting on some rocks on my local beach and, while I'm catching some spray every now and again, I'm not wet and will be able to continue to write here. That's only because the high tide today is 4.4m (We're five days away from full moon). The highest I've seen it is 6.3m and if I'd been sitting here then I'd be very wet indeed. Low tide is supposedly 2.1m, and yet I've seen a tide here as low as half a metre.

Missing the tide isn't just about timing, it's about timing in relation to the outcome. If you knew nothing about sailing you might guess that missing the tide meant missing high tide, and yet I'd suggest that if you waited that long you'd be too late most of the time.

Earlier I asked what was the preferred tide height, and now I ask when that will happen, remembering that some surges only happen at spring tides.

Lindisfarne in Northumbria is a tidal island, with the sea cutting the island off from the mainland at high tide. Every year numerous vehicle drivers ignore the warnings and drive across at the wrong time; they get stuck midway across and have to retreat to the safety station on foot, leaving their vehicle to the mercy of the tide. There are guidelines that specify two safe crossing times per day and, while

I'm sure there's actually more leeway than the guidelines admit to (after all, it can't be good one minute and not the next), it is preferable that visitors drive over during the safe periods stated.

That said, there are times of year when there's a particularly low high tide and the road is never covered with water. It's important to understand when these times are; and the prevailing wind has to be considered, as this might jeopardize the crossing even with such a low high tide.

In this instance missing the tide is a good thing in that it presupposes inaction, because missing the tide here would mean not getting stuck in the water and so not needing to be airlifted to safety.

### Could not pushing ahead have been a good thing in this situation?

Of course, your situation could be related to the tide without it being about missing it. I've a laughter-filled LYL vlog that uses the tide as an example of its predictability too. You can rely on the tide to be a tide – it's not a tree, it's not a flower, it's not sun or rain, it's a tide.

It's no use complaining about the tide being high because you know it's going to be that height at least two times if not four times a day (this depends where in the tide you're measuring).

In what way are you expecting more of someone or yourself than you, or they, are able to deliver? Of course we'd sometimes like people to change, or be different, but we can't start complaining when their actions are consistent with previous actions.

There's another vlog of the tide lapping against the sea wall. The longer I deliberate about when to walk in front of the sea wall, the higher the tide rises and the less likely I am to be able to walk there without getting my feet wet. A great example that sometimes the time is now – not in another minute but now!

I remember on one particular visit, standing here in Burntisland at a low tide of half a metre, and realizing that in about six and a half hours' hours' time there would be over four metres of water above my head. A very scary thought, and perhaps something that supports the premise throughout this chapter that timing is everything. It would be easy to drown if I stayed where I was; therefore I needed to keep moving with the tide back to high-tide mark. Staying too long at low tide is not great, whereas staying beyond high tide is very safe.

Although as the famous saying goes, boats are not meant to stay in harbour but go out to sea!

Missing the tide does depend on where you are in relation to the tide too – on top of it in a boat, swimming in the water or walking on the beach.

If the tide brought with it huge waves that knocked down everything in its path, then missing the tide would be a good thing. If the sea was more like a millpond and you wanted to go surfing, then perhaps not. A great reminder that the state of the sea needs to be appropriate to the action you want to take in relation to it.

The sea is a force to be reckoned with and certainly respected. You'd never go sailing without first understanding how to sail a boat, and to do that you'd have learned about the sea. Forecasting the weather is very important – knowing if the conditions are right for what we want to do. How many trips have been postponed due to weather fronts appearing just as the sailors wanted to set off? The sailors know that waiting will save them time – and possibly, in the long run, their lives. Far better to wait out the storm and only set out when conditions are favourable.

What insights have come as you've explored the landscape you were describing? Had you really missed the tide? What changes have you made to either the saying or your constructed image?

As you now reflect on the original situation, what do you notice? As you leave the metaphor behind and reflect on real life, what actions do you need to take place? And when will you take them?

You have now completed your exploration of all the sayings in this book that keep us stuck.

The final chapter deals with going with the flow. Going with the flow ensures that you avoid any further mishaps and keeps you on track. There is, however, a caveat: sometimes going with the flow can take you up the creek, or into a rut; attention is needed to ensure that flow takes you instead towards your desired outcome.

# CHAPTER 14

# GOING WITH THE FLOW –
# WHERE IS YOUR ALIVENESS?

The premise throughout this whole book is that we need to release barriers to progress to enable us to get back on track.

For most of the other sayings in the book the phrase is the problem, or the barrier to progress, but exploring the phrase will also provide solutions as to how to get out of it. For example, when you're stuck in a rut you just have to find ways to get out of the rut, or if you've got your head in the sand you just need to take your head out of the sand.

Going with the flow is a little different.

Going with the flow is not generally seen as a problem; in some ways it is the aim of this book: to go with the flow at all times, and make decisions that further support you heading in that direction.

The challenge is that many of us go with the flow but still end up in a rut, not being able to see the wood for the trees, and so on.

This chapter is therefore about ensuring when you're going with the flow that it's going to support you, not hinder you.

Let's first ascertain that going against the flow is not desirable.

Remember we're thinking metaphorically; to embody the words, we can imagine being the water in a river where flow is going towards the ocean. It's essential that we put to the back of our mind that we're a human being wanting to buck the system, and to go against conventional wisdom. I'm with you on not wanting to do what other people tell me I have to do – I really do empathize. In nature, however, when you are water, then going with the flow is the only thing to do!

The aim is to also stick with the metaphor. Getting out of the water would change the situation, and there would be no flow. We're not changing the saying to "flying high" or "using bridges" (burnt or otherwise). We're just going to stick with going with the flow for now.

Going against the flow is impossible for water – which might explain why it's never going to get us to our desired outcome. Even if we become a fish in the water, or a duck on it, going against the flow is hard work and involves going backwards. It is also fighting against an inevitable outcome – you might be able to go against the flow for so long, but sooner or later you'll get carried away back downstream by the power of the flow.

The cycle of water starts with water landing, as rain, high in the mountains, and then flowing all the way to the ocean via streams and rivers.

In this instance going with the flow is therefore a positive action, and any outcome other than the ocean is not preferred. Flow towards the ocean is our aim, and any other flow is only an illusion of progress.

I know this may sound weird but that's because we're just used to using this phrase but not thinking about the impact it is having on our feelings, thoughts and actions. If the risk is that we can go with the flow and end up in places we don't want to be, then continuing to explore the phrase metaphorically might just provide some solutions. Stick with me.

The challenge then becomes about the illusions we thought meant we were going with the flow. After all, how come many of us go with the flow and yet still end up feeling like we're:

- Stuck in the mud
- Up the creek without a paddle
- Caught up in a whirlpool
- Dammed up
- Sinking
- Drowning
- Swamped
- Stagnant

- At a dead end
- Buffeted by everything around us

In other words, we end up stuck – again!

Bear in mind the full meaning of the phrase: it's only going with the flow when it's headed towards the ocean. Which means that if we end up somewhere else we shouldn't be surprised if the outcome isn't to our liking.

The aim is to ensure that the flow we're following is ocean-bound; and in order to understand the answer to that question we have to become a river or stream.

At any moment the flow of a river can split, and the water go off in many different directions. The water that doesn't end up in the ocean might do so because it went instead in the direction where the most energy was, or where was easier or required less effort. After all, "going with the flow" sounds easy, certainly not as if it requires proactive action.

Intuition, our innate intelligence, will help determine our route – the key is in asking the question of our intuition about our current direction, and then noticing the different decision points when we need to ask this question of ourselves.

At every fork in the metaphorical river we need to ask ourselves which one is headed for the ocean, and take that one. This constant refining of your path or flow is not achieved through passivity – in fact, I'm just looking at my affirmation app on my phone and today's affirmation could so easily be about flow and water:

I persevere. I am relentless. I persist. I keep going.

I'd add an additional sentence to that:

I persevere. I am relentless. I persist. I keep going. I listen to my intuition.

The biggest challenge is in realizing where all the decision points are, remembering that the only person to be able to determine your route to the ocean is YOU and listening to that whispering voice inside that knows your route. You are the navigator, and in every moment of every day you are guiding yourself towards the ocean, in the smallest of course corrections, corrections that will allow you to benefit from the flow with ease and effortlessness.

So far we've stayed with the metaphor, and normally at this point we would move on to applying what we've learned about the saying to the current situation. In this instance, though, I don't think that would be helpful; we'd get caught up in determining what represents the ocean, and potentially end up stuck in the mud anyway.

For example, we might think that sending our CV to ten employment agencies will be helpful when we want to find job A in area B. That is, we've defined the goal as being finding a specific job in a specific area. In this instance, we'd all agree that sending our CV to employment agencies would help us achieve our goal.

However, we might still end up stuck. We end up stuck because we've asked ourselves the wrong question – which in the above example is "What do I need to do to send out CVs to ten employment agencies?"

Here's how to avoid that.

We instead ask ourselves "Will sending an email today to ten employment agencies help me get to the ocean?", to which the answer might be "No." I know that might sound odd but trust me, your unconscious will provide you with an answer, and we don't really need to understand why – just that the answer is "No."

The task then is to find out what action would keep you headed for the ocean – which *might* be:

- Taking time out first to just be.
- Deciding what difference you want to make in the world – your contribution.
- Talking to your partner about when you start a family.
- Talking to your now adult children about when they're leaving home.

- Redefining the location you want the job to be in.
- Redefining the job you want.
- Understanding your current financial situation.
- Finding out what you could do with your skills.
- Learning new skills.
- Or simply updating your CV before you send the email.

In other words, finding out the precise action needed to be taken next will ensure that you keep heading for the ocean; and, more importantly, help you avoid the dead ends – after all, what a waste of time sending the ten emails, and responding to queries, and even attending interviews, if your heart isn't really in it, or you were very grumpy as you went through the process, with no access to your communication skills. These kinds of things might have been avoided by, say, going on holiday first so you were rested before you started.

If you're still unsure about this unconscious "yes"/"no" malarkey, try it for yourself and see.

Think of two situations – one you know to be on track, and one you know to be off track. Now ask this question of each of the situations:

"Am I headed for the ocean?"

The answer may come as a yes or no, a stop or go sign, the colours red or green, an image of an ocean or being up the creek… Or the answer may come as a physical sensation (yes for me is a straight head, no is off to the left). In other words, you may need to test it a few times till you're sure of how your yes and no are communicated.

Did you get the answer you expected with respect to those two situations?

If not, just check these are both situations that you definitely, absolutely know to be currently either on or off track. You might want to try something easier for the purposes of this trial – maybe asking about eating a food you know you like versus one that upsets your stomach. Not necessarily things that stop you getting to the ocean, but things nonetheless that can hinder you.

Just play about with asking this question until you're comfortable with how you get a yes or no response. In other words, you don't need to have determined what the ocean is to know whether an action is the right one or not in the current situation.

Once you can interpret your yes/no then start asking the question "Am I headed for, or will this take me to, the ocean?" for daily decisions you make, and just notice what you notice.

Going with the flow is not passive; neither is it accepting the status quo. It is it about making intentional decisions based on the answer to the question "Am I headed for, or will this take me to, the ocean?"

It is important to keep on asking the question. The flow of a mountain stream is a very different beast to the flow of a mighty river, or the flow of water as it reaches the ocean. What worked when we were a small stream may no longer work once we're a river.

Water keeps flowing forward constantly. Lots of time out, thinking about things, isn't really what going with the flow is all about. Bodies of water by their very nature have slower and quicker parts and balance is already inherent in the saying. So too is constant progress. That said, if the answer to "Is doing nothing at this time still enabling me to go to the ocean?" is yes, then all is well. The challenge is knowing when the doing-nothing sort of going with the flow is taking you in a less helpful or even downright wrong direction. I'd suggest asking "Is doing nothing for a week/month/season taking me to the ocean?" to check, or regularly asking yourself the question "Am I headed for the ocean?" Either of these will help you avoid the mud!

That said, perseverance, relentlessness and persistence can be tiring; you may want to make one of your decisions the decision to aim for the edge of the stream and take it a little slower until the rain comes to pick you up and carry you back into the main flow. This, crucially, is not about stopping but about making slower progress.

In order to go with the flow, those control freaks among us must release our resistance to letting external forces determine our speed and general direction. Some control is maintained by keeping our path aligned with the ocean – fine-tuning the day-to-day speed and direction of flow that allows our values and all we treasure in life to be achieved. We write the plan even if the destination is a given.

Fear can also hinder us in going with the flow – it is easy to become fearful, pulling back from the energy of the flow fearing we'll end up alone, hurt, in the wrong place and so on. It's important to remember that as long as we stay aligned with the ocean, all will be very well.

Fear can also be a constant companion when faced, for example, with rapids or a waterfall. We must remember however that the objective is the ocean, and these rapids, or this waterfall, are simply one step along the way towards that ocean. Unless you can see an alternative, then sooner or later you will be taken through this part of the flow. Resistance will tire you out and make the journey through the rapids harder. The answer really is to go with the flow, open your heart and trust that all is well, and know you really are headed for the ocean. You are the water – and water loves rapids and waterfalls and knows precisely how to navigate them.

Interestingly, the more water there is the greater the flow. Which means collaboration with others is a given in this metaphor. It isn't about competition, just about joining others who have a similar goal.

However, going with the flow is not about clinging to others, or following them without discernment. It's okay as long as the answer to the question "Am I headed for the ocean?" is yes. However, their ocean might be a different ocean to yours, so don't let yourself be carried away by or with those around you and then miss the opportunity to make the decision to take a different route.

Discernment requires vigilance about making choices. Be very aware of the behaviours that stop us achieving the appropriate level of vigilance. These behaviours are those that consume your mind and prevent you from noticing a decision point. Behaviours such as negativity, jealousy and anger. Openness and positivity are a great antidote to these, and will help you make those course corrections that stop you from drifting off course or even drowning.

Like anything we learn, initially this will all require vigilance, and a very conscious decision to ask the question "Am I headed for the ocean?", possibly many times daily. After a while though this skill will slip into your unconscious, and the small course corrections that keep you on track and afloat will be made without you even thinking about it.

This exploration is not only useful if you're not achieving what you want in life.

If you're happy and have everything you want, and are doing what you enjoy, then I'd suggest that you already are in the flow. This technique may, though, still help you by keeping you going with the flow, on track and headed for the ocean.

It's important you don't mix the metaphor and real life, otherwise you might end up stuck again.

Denise knew the decision to take her current job had taken her up the creek. She thought therefore that getting back into flow meant she had to decide what job she did want. That then sent her into not being able to see the wood for the trees!

I realized as we talked that being in the flow includes making these sorts of decisions, but also changing your mind, and all the other "mess" of life. As long as you're headed for the ocean, that's what matters.

In this example Denise had been going with the flow but the decision to take this job took her up the creek. Deciding she needed a different job got her back into flow. The challenge was then in how to make decisions based on keeping her headed for the ocean. She didn't need to know what job – just that she wanted a different one and to start to pull an action plan together using the question "Am I headed for the ocean?" to help develop that plan.

Part 3 of the book provides additional assistance in exploring your imagined landscapes, and a very quick process to use if you would like a different perspective and have limited time.

PART 3

# LAST THOUGHTS

# CHAPTER 15

# A QUICK FIX — ADVICE FROM AN UNSTUCK YOU

This section is for you if: you resonate with one of the sayings used in the book; don't have time to do any of the exercises outlined here; and want a different perspective on a problem you're facing – NOW.

I obtained the advice here by imagining myself doing a little time travel! To do that, I imagined moving to a time in the future when I was no longer set back in the way described by each of the sayings. I then asked myself what advice I would give that younger and stuck me, that could move me forward.

For example:

- I then asked myself what advice I would give that younger and stuck me, which could move me forward.
- I considered what that future self would say, if I couldn't see the wood for the trees, to help me turn the corner to enable me to get a different perspective, or
- I imagined what it would be like to have found a sense of direction and to have stopped going round in circles and have put an end to all that dizziness.

First decide which of the following sayings best describes the current situation you'd benefit from a different perspective on:

- Stuck in a rut
- Can't see the wood for the trees
- Up the creek without a paddle
- Like a fish out of water
- Head in the sand
- Out on a limb
- Going round in circles
- Treading water
- Missed the tide

From the antidotes below, simply pick the one that is needed to solve your current challenge, and read the advice given.

You may find one of the pieces of advice provides the necessary perspective; or perhaps you need to read them all to get that; or while reading them your mind may go off on a different tangent, and it turns out to be that tangent that provides the solution. You may even find that an antidote from a different saying also helps. The key is to allow your subconscious to help you experience a different perspective, and therefore obtain insight about what action to take next.

Here's the advice I gave myself:

## Out of the Rut (for when you're stuck in a rut)

The rut has become too familiar, and you've simply forgotten what it's like to be on track. Being back on track can also become a familiar feeling, and one that is accompanied by health, well-being and laughter too. Remember something you are on track about, and allow that sense of direction and purpose to expand into the current situation.

More ease, and less tension and trying. Before taking any further action do something to release the tension – that may involve running; having a relaxing bath; doing a crossword or puzzle; or perhaps (this is my new hobby) going for a very refreshing open-water swim in the sea! Anything that enables you to access a more relaxed state of mind and body.

The first step is simple. Trust you have walked this way before, and can do so again. Take the first step with confidence, and don't look back.

### Can See the Wood for the Trees (for when you can't see the wood for the trees)

You just need to stand back, and not be so intense. Don't try to do it all at once.

The wood is such a small part of the grand scheme of the journey. Don't make it the journey. In fact, any direction you take will be a good one because it will get you moving – any direction travelled in with conviction will get you there. And you can make course corrections as you go. It's the wavering that means you go in one direction and then return to the start, unsure whether that was the right way to go.

There are 360 degrees of choice, and they're all preferable to the static stuck choice you're making at the moment.

### Paddle in Hand and No Longer up the Creek (for when you're up the creek without a paddle)

You're going nowhere; indecision is keeping you stuck. Just decide what to do, and do it.

Any movement will be in the right direction – it's inaction that's keeping you stuck.

Don't allow the saying to constrain the solution – finding a paddle isn't necessarily the only solution. For example, the water isn't that deep. Can you wade out, swim out, float out?

### A Fish Swimming in Water (for when you're like a fish out of water)

Going back into the water is not failure, it's essential for your survival. Once in the water, it will be much, much easier to find the options, opportunities and solutions.

Remember it's not as far as you think, or as long out of the water; it just feels like it.

You can do it. Just keep calm and persevere.

### Head out of the Sand (for when you've got your head in the sand – or others are suggesting you have)

So much wasted time and energy while you have your head down rather than up. So many opportunities that are passing you by that you can't see because you aren't looking.

So much unnecessary effort is required to keep your head down even when you can hear interesting sounds and other people passing. Just take your head out of the sand; and take time to allow the blood to flow around your body easily and effortlessly and notice what opportunities exist.

Head up, open your eyes, look around and breathe.

### Off the Limb (for when you're feeling like you're well and truly out on a limb)

What can you do to make coming off the limb more palatable – what would make it safer?

Jump. It's easier than you think, and it's a lot less scary than you think the other side of letting go.

Being stuck in a state of fear is depleting your energy and creativity. Let go, and the energy and creativity will be there again.

### No Longer Going Round in Circles (for when you're dizzy from going round in circles)

If you keep doing what you've always done you'll keep getting what you've always got. Change direction; go round in squares; slow down your circling; speed it up; or make it a bigger or smaller circle. Do something different, and notice how that allows a different outcome.

Remember to look for the insight in the situation – why this circle, why now, why here? What lesson do you need to learn from this situation for it to release its magnetic hold on you?

So much wasted time for fear of making a wrong decision. Just follow your gut, and trust that all that you fear losing will either be given to you again, or will be replaced with something even greater.

Your gut doesn't choose a direction because it thinks it will give you less of what you have now; it makes a choice for more and greater. Dishonouring your intuition stops the muscle from working, and makes it harder to hear – honour and listen so that you may be stronger in the end.

## Swimming Comfortably, or Out of Water (for when you're treading water)

Float, and just gather your energy and look around you before you take the next stroke out of there!

There are times when not moving is the best option, but you've missed so many opportunities because you have an ideal scenario of what you want life to be like. The perfection of your dreams is not a realistic outcome. Let go of perfection, and know that commitment to doing your best is more than enough.

Stop wearing yourself out; let go and trust that all will be very well; and allow the water's flow to take you in the right direction.

## Caught the Tide (for when you're disappointed at having missed the tide)

There are never times when you can't get there – just times when it's harder, and times when it's easier.

Waiting for perfection can sap your energy, and makes the journey much harder than it needs to be. It also makes the journey greyer and certainly longer. Imagine a more colourful outcome, and notice what you notice.

Yes, some preparation is needed, but only the essentials – it isn't about being 100% prepared for 100% of all eventualities. It's about being more prepared for the ones with the highest impact or biggest likelihood of happening (as those with the lowest impact won't matter, and those with the lowest likelihood of happening are unlikely to happen).

## Going with the Flow (for when you've been stuck in any of the above situations)

Ease and flow. Less is more.

No past, no history, no future – attention in the moment, allowing you to get a sense of when to float, when to act and when to stop.

Remember these insights came from my own future self, advising me on what to do when I had been using the saying to describe a situation. The advice may have resonated for you too. The advice may also not have resonated – in which case you may want to ask your own future self for some advice; that future you who has already resolved the problem you're trying to sort out. Give it a try!

One suggestion: I've found it's best to either say the advice out loud (perhaps recording it as you do) or write it as if your future self is writing a letter to your current self.

Good luck – you don't really need it though. The solution is already known to a part of you – you just need to listen to that part, that inner you that is wise beyond all logical understanding.

# CHAPTER 16

# QUESTIONS TO EXPLORE YOUR METAPHORICAL LANDSCAPE

Throughout the book I've held your hand, metaphorically at least, as we've explored the landscapes contained within the sayings. It's that exploration, and the different perspectives obtained, that have provided you with possible solutions to get back on track.

You might have been surprised to see that finding a solution within your imaginary landscape means it's much easier for your mind to find a solution in real life. For example, realizing that you need a map to get out of the wood might have prompted you to become clearer about the steps you needed to take to get from where you are in a situation to where you want to be.

Me writing this book is a great example of this for me – simply adding "Write the book" on to my to-do list kept me going round in circles and I certainly couldn't see the wood for the trees. Which resulted in me going nowhere fast.

It was only when I made a list breaking "Write the book" down into all its component parts, and could see the map and the route I needed to take, that progress was made. Once I had made the list, I could identify what free time I had available, and what would get written when.

Each of the chapters here has provided a small number of potential solutions to the saying in question. They are not an exhaustive exploration of the landscape contained within the saying; they simply outline some common themes I've observed over the last 20 years. You may, therefore, have yet to discover the ultimate solution, and that's where this chapter comes in.

This chapter will guide you on a deeper exploration of your metaphorical landscape.

For example, noticing that it is the rain that's stopping you from seeing the wood for the trees might be hugely insightful. However, unless I ask you the question about the weather in your landscape, you may not realize that this is the difference that's going to make the difference.

Why it might make a difference will be unique to everyone reading this book. For example, imagine that you're embarking on a journey, and you're standing there in the great outdoors and it starts to rain, perhaps a cold rain, and it rains for hours and hours and hours. How enthusiastic would you be to start out on your journey? Many of us, I suspect, would head back indoors and wait for the rain to stop.

In our imagination, where we can't see the wood for the trees, the rain might be having the same impact as it would in the example above. It's as if the rain is draining all life out of us, and killing what motivation we might have.

The LYL process suggests that taking the rain out of our imaginary landscape might help us find the clarity we've been lacking in real life. Just like the sun that has come out as I type this, and has started to glint on the sea, and is inviting me to go for a swim.

This section, therefore, provides you with different questions to help you explore the landscape, or the saying you're using, in order to understand it more fully and therefore uncover the solutions that are currently eluding you – perhaps because they're hidden by the onset of rain.

I've divided the questions into two areas:

- Changing the words used to describe the saying itself.
- Changing what we see, feel, hear, taste and smell in the landscape, and then moving around it.

The list of questions is not exhaustive, and is just for you to get a better sense of how to explore a landscape. Once you're familiar with the process you'll often be able to explore the landscape without reference to these questions.

If you're describing a particularly stuck state, I'd suggest this list may help because it may remind you of something that would make a difference. For example, I always forget to play around with the soundtrack to my internal images, and yet for me adding a soundtrack so often shifts a situation!

The first set of questions is about going absurd and having some fun with the saying you're using.

## Change the Saying

Absurdity is a technique to shift mindsets and ways of thinking – especially a stuck mindset – because it sends us into something called a trans-derivational search. That is, we go into our mind trying to make sense of what's just been said. The absurdity of it makes us laugh, and at the same time allows a shift in perspective.

One way of doing that here is to play around with the saying – so, rather than not seeing the wood for the trees you might be up the creek without a tree instead. The idea is to get as playful as possible.

Here are some suggestions that may just shift your brain out of its comfort zone and take you down, or perhaps up or round, a different direction. In so doing, they may help you to find the solution that's been eluding you.

### Making Mountains out of Molehills

- Making hills out of molehills
- Making clouds out of mist
- Making woods out of trees
- Making forests out of woods
- Making a storm out of a shower
- Making a molehill out of a rut

Do try some of your own – your own mind wants to help you too. Since it understands the current situation very well, it may provide just the right example to make you laugh, and so get an additional or different perspective on the situation in hand.

Here are some more:

- Climbing mountains out of molehills
- Moulding mountains out of molehills
- Moulding molehills out of mountains
- Compressing mountains into molehills

This is a great game to play with other people – as I have found while writing my own list here, it's easy to run out of steam doing it alone. You could have prizes for who can get the most absurd!

### Stuck in a Rut

- Stuck out of a rut
- Stuck in a wood
- Unstuck in a rut
- Stuck in a valley
- Can't see the rut for the mud!

You will notice that I can think of more suggestions for some of the sayings than others. I'm sure each time you, or I, return to this section we'll think of more suggestions. I'd highly recommend, therefore, that you make a note of those additional ideas, for future reference.

- Like a rut out of the mud
- Missed the rut
- Going round in ruts (this is the one that made me chuckle today)

## Can't See the Wood for the Trees

- Can't see the trees for the wood
- Can't see the wood for the forest
- Can't see the bark for the trees
- Can't see the trees for the bark
- Can't see the trees for the sound of the bark
- Like a tree out of a wood
- Can't see the rut for the mud
- Stuck in a tree
- Up a creek without a tree
- Can't see the wood for the creek
- And so on – the more absurd the better

Remember the aim is to change the internal representation you have for the situation – once you've done that then you're on your way from being stuck to getting back on track, or even going with the flow – if that isn't too many metaphors.

- Can't see the forest for the trees
- Can't see the forest for the wood
- Can't hear the birds for the song
- Can't see the stream for the rain
- Can't feel the wind for the storm
- Can't see the fish for the water
- Can't see the rut for the leaves
- Can't see the castle for the sand

Did any of these make you laugh or resonate at some level? Perhaps they jarred you out of your sense of stuckness with an "Of course, how remiss of me, I know what I need to do now!"

The aim at all times is to notice when you're no longer feeling quite as stuck as you were when you started, and that a potential solution has possibly emerged. What these processes are doing is allowing our subconscious – which knows the answer – to nudge us via the metaphor in the direction of the solution.

### Up the Creek Without a Paddle

- Up the estuary without a paddle
- Up the creek without an engine
- Up the creek without a boat
- Up the river without a paddle
- On the beach without a paddle
- In the canoe/boat without a paddle
- Between a burning bridge and a paddleless boat
- Sailing too close to the burning bridge

### Feel Like a Fish out of Water

- Feel like a fish out of sparkling water (this makes me laugh every time I read it)
- Feel like a fish out of mud
- Feel like a fish out of rain
- Feel like a fish in water
- Feel like a pig in mud
- Feel like a pig out of mud
- Feel like a fish out of air
- Feel like a flying fish out of water
- Feel like an amphibious fish out of water
- Feel like a rut out of water
- Feel like a wood out of water
- Feel like a circle out of a square

### Head in the Sand

- Head in the air
- Head in the clouds
- Head up a mountain
- Head out of a molehill

Oh dear, I ran out of ideas very quickly here – perhaps I'm too easily affiliated with head in the sand! This is a great reminder that it can be a good idea to get others to help us explore the sayings we're using.

- Head on a limb
- Sand on the limb
- Head in a sandcastle
- Head and body in the sand
- Head in a bucket and spade
- Head in a hole
- Head up for air

## Out on a Limb

- On a limb
- In on a limb
- Out on a branch
- In on a branch
- Out on a tree
- In a tree
- Out on a wave
- Out on a rut
- Out on an arm
- Out on a leg
- Up on a limb
- Down on a limb
- Right on a limb
- Left on a limb
- Out on a thick branch
- Out on a trunk
- Out on my limb
- Out on an unbreakable limb
- Out on a mountain
- Out on a creek
- Out on a tree
- A fish on a limb
- A mole on a limb
- Up a creek without a limb
- Out on a creek's limb

I said I could think of more ideas for some sayings than others...

### In at the Deep End

- Out at the deep end
- In at the shallow end
- In at the deep beginning
- In at the shallow beginning
- Out at the shallow end
- Out at the long end
- Out at the short end

### Going Round in Circles

- Going round anticlockwise
- Going round clockwise
- Going round in squares/triangles/octagons etc
- Going square in circles
- Going round in watery circles
- Going round in muddy circles
- Going round in grassy circles
- Going back round
- Going round in broken circles
- Going round in spheres

### Treading Water

- Drinking water
- Wading water
- Throwing water
- Treading the boards
- Treading the mill
- Treading glasses of water
- Treading the waves
- Treading the wet stuff

- Swimming in one place
- Treading treacle/molasses (although I suspect that might be what it feels like – but for some of you this may just be the different perspective you were needing – after all, isn't it so much easier to float on treacle? or what about custard!)

## Missed the Tide

- Mist the tide
- Caught the tide
- Narrowly missed the tide
- Missed the bus
- Missed the high tide
- Missed the higher tide
- Missed the highest tide
- Missed the low tide
- Missed the spring tide
- Missed the turning tide
- Missed a high low tide
- Missed the fish out of water
- Missed a low high tide
- Caught the tide
- Caught the low high tide
- Ignored the tide
- Loved the tide
- Moved the tide

Remember the aim is to play lightly with this process. If it starts to feel heavy or hard then go and do something else. This is best undertaken as a game, where the silliest suggestion wins the prize, rather than trying to find the cleverest idea!

You can of course do this for any saying you're using to describe your current stuck state. Mix it, move it, shake it all about and allow yourself to experience the situation differently.

## Questions about the Landscape

Before I jump in with the questions for you to think about, I want to remind you why we're asking these questions, and why making changes to the image you have of the landscape will help.

Think of an evening out, perhaps with friends or family, when you had a great time. What did you see, hear and feel? Remember who was with you – perhaps recall what they were wearing or what they were doing. Recall the sounds. Remember how you were feeling and what you were doing. Relive it as if it was happening now.

How does that make you feel?

Think of another situation that you didn't enjoy at all – one that made you sad, perhaps, angry or annoyed. Again, recall everything about that situation.

How do you feel?

The likelihood is you will feel differently after recalling each of these events. Despite the fact that neither of these events is happening now, they both still have the ability to impact how you're feeling.

You can also make them better or worse – by, for example, altering the representation – taking out colour or adding it in, changing the people, their facial expressions, what was being said or done... You can try associating or disassociating from the memory.

The point is that you can change how you feel by changing the representation you have.

That's where we're going with this process. The aim throughout the book has been to take a constructed and imagined landscape that metaphorically represents a stuck state, and to somehow change it so that you are no longer stuck.

There are a number of ways of doing this, but the key is to always stay within the metaphor for as long as possible. For example, you shouldn't decide that the paddle you lost when you were up the creek represents you losing other people, and then decide you didn't need them anyway.

That's the whole reason for sticking with the metaphor, with the saying and landscape, for as long as possible: you can keep everyday beliefs and judgements to one side while you explore the patterns within the situation, patterns that will ultimately provide you with a clue as to where the solution lies.

Throughout the book we have looked at exploring the landscape in a variety of ways – through drawing a map or a picture of the landscape, or visiting a landscape that best represents the saying for you; plotting a course towards an alternate landscape; or changing the image.

The aim has been to describe the current landscape fully, and then change the image so that you no longer feel stuck and instead can access ideas as to what to do next.

The following questions will help you understand just what a broad range of landscape characteristics we can change.

Remember, when Jen couldn't see the wood for the trees she changed the type of trees to beech, which made all the difference and inspired immediate action. In other words, play around with the image. By simply making changes to an image we've constructed, we make changes to the situation we feel stuck in or have an issue with. As in this example, sometimes you only need to make one change.

This will never be an exhaustive list of questions, by the way; it's simply a small selection to give you a sense of the possible.

Basically, we're looking to describe the landscape using our senses, or modalities:

- What can we see
- What can we hear
- What can we feel
- What can we taste
- What can we smell

We all have preferences as to how we remember and construct images in our mind. The solutions may be found in our preferred modality, or in one we don't often use. That is – you may be able to describe every visual aspect of the landscape, but only find the solution when asked to change the temperature; or you may just need to see the summer sun in the sky.

We are all different – even my preferences will impact the breadth of examples I give here, as well as those I've given in earlier chapters. Editors and friends may expand my examples – but they'll only add their own preferences to mine!

These preferences are also impacted by the landscape we choose, no one landscape being either the same or easily understood by others. I can't see your sea, only my own interpretation of it, and the real sea as I look out of my window as I type this, or when I go to the beach.

There is a saying that there are always three versions of a story – yours, mine and the truth. In this instance, we're trying to get to neither the truth nor my interpretation of it but to explore yours. Of course, my analysis may help to provide clues to what might help you – but then again it may not. Changing the time of day may make a huge difference to me, and make no difference to you at all. We can certainly use the actual landscape to provide prompts, but again they're only ever going to be a prompt – we're dealing with a constructed image that's in your mind, that to all intents and purposes may use different laws of nature from nature itself.

Although a word or warning! If your landscape is defying normal laws of nature, please consider what happens if you apply the laws rather than ignore them.

I worked with someone once who was metaphorically able to easily live on the moon. In real life, they saw themselves as very much an outsider and were unable to relate to others. At the time, I went with their landscape, but in hindsight I would have challenged that idea, as it was just another way for them to easily remain an outsider and not resolve issues they were having with everyone in their life.

I've yet to be convinced that a non-Earthly landscape works as a long-term strategy. Mainly because my experience is we need fire, water, air and earth for a landscape to be sustainable. Lunar landscapes won't have this – neither will they have lots of people, and I'm unsure that hiding from the world to that extent is healthy.

I think it's the same with ignoring the normal passage of the seasons – spring being followed by summer, autumn and winter. That is, having the seasons out of sequence. If, however, you're very sure that in your landscape there is no spring or autumn, and that winter moves straight into summer, then consider what longitude or latitude that may require.

For example, when I worked with someone who was in a desert and wanted more rain in the landscape, rather than go in the direction they thought they would need to, they found they needed to move their landscape into the tropics – i.e., towards the equator and not away from it – a huge insight at the time.

While not ideal, becoming an animal instead of human may provide more insight. Occasionally, in order for our imagination to make meaning, it may be helpful to disassociate completely from the landscape, especially when feeling like a fish out of water. It may also give us the perspective we need. So:

- Would being a seabird help if you've missed the tide?
- Or a beaver when you're stuck by a logjam?
- Would a badger or a mole see the wood for the trees differently?
- What would a frog think about the rut?
- What would a heron think of the fish out of water?

Here's a starter for ten of the types of characteristics for you to consider as you reflect on your landscape, noticing what you notice as you answer the questions and deciding as you do whether changing the answer, and the constructed landscape you have for a saying, will move you away from being stuck or get you even more stuck.

The only rule, if there is one, is to put the real situation to one side for as long as possible. If at all possible identify the situation; score it; and then put it in a box to open again later. Don't keep opening the box to check how the metaphor might apply.

Remember, not every question will relate to your landscape, and even if it does your answer might be "I don't know" or "I don't care." Store these answers in case the solution lies in knowing or caring but, for the time being, answer the questions that do relate to the imaginary landscape you can see, imagine, hear or feel.

What you're aiming for is:

- Seeing the sights – colours, shapes, focus, contrast.
- Hearing the sounds – natural and man-made, the rhythm and pitch of the sound, the direction it's coming from.

- Feeling the feelings – the temperature, the wind in your hair or body, the ground underfoot (hard/soft; even/uneven; gradient), the air you breathe in and out.
- Smelling or tasting the landscape – which won't make sense for everyone but for some might just make the difference they need.
- Noticing the movements – tide, leaves, animals and insects.
- Noticing the weather, or time of year.

### Questions to Consider about the Image and the Landscape Contained within it

- Where is your attention drawn to –the trees or the bark, the path or the horizon, the sky or the leaves underfoot?
- What is the longitude and latitude of the landscape?
- Is the image in 2D or 3D?
- Is it in colour? Black and white? Grey?
- Is the image moving or still?
- Are you associated with the picture (looking through your eyes) or disassociated (you can see yourself in the image)?
- Does your landscape have sounds – yes/no, soft/loud, a particular type of rhythm, etc.?
- What are you feeling – for example, the temperature?
- Where is the image of the landscape located – in front of you, to the side, in your mind etc.?
- What is the size of the image – lifesize, smaller than lifesize, bigger etc.?
- None of these?
- All of these?
- Something else entirely?

There's no right or wrong question or answer. Just questions that feel like they're taking you even more up the creek, and questions that bring more clarity to the scene, and help you get back on track. Please don't be constrained by this list; they are a small sample of the potential questions that could be asked about your landscape. As you look and listen, and experience your imagined landscape, what other descriptions could you provide? Perhaps if you're up the creek without a paddle:

- What time of day/season/year is it?
- Describe the weather.
- If the creek is in the sea, are there waves, and if so what height and power?
- How would you describe the current?
- What about the water temperature?
- Or the wind speed or wind direction?
- Is the water deep or shallow?

You may get insight just from describing the landscape.

To release the sense of stuckness (whatever that means for you) you may however need to make changes to it. With the guiding principle being that, if any changes make the landscape feel more stuck, change it back again, and notice what changes you can make that feel like you're back on track and in the flow.

Changes can be made by changing any aspects of the landscape and might, to use "Can't see the wood for the trees" as an example, include:

- Adding more or less colour, or even making the image black and white.
- Changing the size of the image.
- Changing the location of the image.
- Zooming in or out.
- Making it more or less focused.
- Making it into a movie, allowing you to explore the landscape more fully.
- Adding sounds – or turning them down.
- Changing the weather.
- Changing the time of day.
- Changing the time of year (perhaps noticing what happens as you imagine the wood in winter with no leaves on the trees – unless you've imagined an evergreen tree).

- Making a path longer or shorter or more visible or straighter or bendier, or simply adding more paths.
- Adding or taking away trees.
- Type of trees – remember Jen felt better as soon as the trees were changed to beech trees (she suddenly felt able to breathe, having felt very stressed and panicky previously).
- Increasing or reducing the size of the trees – which may include their height, circumference or even the number or thickness of branches.
- Moving the location of the wood – what happens if you change it to a wood you know rather than don't or vice versa.
- Or adding some animals – perhaps a wood full of badgers would make it feel better – or what about butterflies!!
- What about the sky – is it blue or cloudy and how does making changes to that help?
- What about changing the location of the sun – at ground level or high in the trees?
- What about the speed with which you're viewing them? As I travelled on a train towards London the other day I realized that I couldn't see the wood OR the trees as it was all too fast. Would slowing down or speeding up your movement help?
- How are you travelling about the landscape – walking, running, car, bridge, boat, zip wire?
- Are the weather conditions in your representation appropriate to the task in hand, and are you appropriately dressed for them? Maybe consider wind strength and direction, pressure (high or low), temperature, rain (gentle or otherwise) and humidity (hail, snow or sleet), the sun's heat, cloud (fluffy white clouds or fog or mist), or weather features such as hurricanes and tornadoes.
- Then there are events such as earthquakes and volcanic eruptions. They may be in the starting landscape, or part of the solution.

When looking to reduce the pain in my arthritic knees, one change in the landscape I imagined involved hardened lava being brought back into the ground via an earthquake to once more make it molten – more pliable and flexible.

- When exploring sunlight we often think of full sun, but of course sun can be filtered through clouds on a continuum from full sunlight to no sunlight. And even no sunlight is cloudy rather than dark. The level of light or dark is therefore another continuum to explore.
- Reflections and shadows are also a great source of insight – have fun amending the levels in the current situation. Does turning it up or down make the most difference?
- Deserts are generally thought of as hot places with no rain, but rain does fall in the desert and it brings lush green shoots of growth. Any landscape can therefore benefit from some rain. Try it and see for yourself – what difference does imagining rain make to your current representation? Remember that the green shoots take some days to appear after the rain; maybe fast-forward your internal movie until you can see the true impact of the rain emerge.
- Your representation may however have very little sun, and so experimenting with the amount, heat and height of the sun in the sky might provide fascinating results.

What you're aiming for is finding a representation that feels better on the level of stuckness and, more importantly, provides you with the capacity to connect to your inner creativity, which will provide numerous potential solutions for you to consider.

- Rain constantly moves, falling on the ground and being absorbed as it moves though the ground into the water table, often joining a stream that ultimately ends up in the ocean. Water holes are important gathering places for animals, just like the coffee machines in our offices are for us – an opportunity for those living on the land to rest and replenish.

- Viewing landscapes through 360 degrees can also be really useful. In one week I managed to see Edinburgh Castle from a number of angles: from my home five miles away; from across the Forth River; from further along the shore on the same side of the Forth; and from above as my plane came in to land at Edinburgh Airport. Each perspective provided more information about the size and shape of, and relationship between, all the elements. Reminding ourselves that we can see things from many angles can help prevent us from determining a future course of action based on just one set of assumptions.
- Would it make a difference if the creek you're imagining was in a different country?

Remember, these questions are ways of looking at the situation metaphorically, which in turn may turn into a realization of the course of action you should take in reality.

For example, imagining a creek in a different country might mean moving it from the middle of South America to just up the road. Can you get a sense of the difference in how you might feel? If you've been treating the current problem as if you're up a creek in the middle of South America, you might find imagining the creek moving to just down the road feels more manageable and less stressful, strange or new (although someone else may find the reverse to be true).

Once the feeling has changed, it will allow your thoughts and actions to follow suit.

Other things to try include:

- Turning 180 degrees or 90 degrees and looking in a different direction.
- Flying through or above the landscape.
- Changing where you are looking – up, down, to the side.
- Would any tools be useful?
- Getting a map or compass out.
- Is the creek you're imagining in a picture or a movie? What happens if you change it from a picture to a movie or vice versa?

- Is it in or out of focus?
- Is it in black and white or colour? What happens if you change it?
- Is there a soundtrack? What happens if you change it?
- Do the sounds need altering – softer/louder?

I may be repeating myself here, but it is worth reintroducing the same idea later as sometimes you can make a change too early, and it doesn't have an impact. That is, you needed to imagine it raining first before you could get the image to change from black and white to colour, or vice versa.

Remember there is no right and wrong – we might think colour would be better than black and white, but not necessarily for you, today, for this situation.

- You can change location – if you move the wood or creek to a different country what other insights do you get?
- What about letting your heart describe the landscape rather than your head – and if you can do so, what about your gut or soul?

This last suggestion might not be an easy exercise for everyone. I include it as an option because it may work for some readers – it certainly does for some of my coaching clients, although not for others. If it doesn't work for you, just let it go and move on to exploring how the other techniques may work for you.

However elaborate some of the above choices, they're not exhaustive and everyone will be able to find a way of changing their landscape not listed above. Remember a metaphor is worth one million words! Don't be surprised therefore if you find you have more ideas than are suggested here. I just hope my examples provide a framework of what's possible for you in order that you can spread your wings and explore.

We will each have different characteristics in our landscapes and these characteristics will have more or less impact on a situation. For example, colour may make a huge difference – positive or negative. Which means I might find myself describing something as getting more colourful and yet it might have more meaning for you if it gets less colourful.

Not wishing to use too many metaphors, finding the right internal representation of a situation is a bit like Goldilocks and the three bears' porridge – not too cold, not too hot, just right. The questions I ask about changing the representation may have no effect, may make it feel worse or make it feel much better.

You always have the option to move the representation back to how it was when you started. The aim is always to make changes to the representation to improve how you're feeling, thus unlocking the door to creativity and all the solutions and opportunities that exist. If the changes you're making aren't doing that then stop and review what's happening for you. What would make it just right? If you ignored my questions, how would you change the representation so it was just right? Not more stuck but back on track and in the flow?

That said, when playing around with these characteristics you may well discount something early on only to find it has meaning later.

You may remember I described earlier in the book asking someone who was treading water if changing the light made a difference, and she said making it lighter made it scarier. So we obviously left the light level as it was. However, once the water was warmer and feet were on the ground, then it became lighter of its own accord. The antidote did require more light, but only after the warmer water, and it did it all by itself.

Thus far we've explored making changes to your constructed landscape. The solution may, however, lie in moving around or out of the current real landscape.

There are many different options for moving about a landscape. Here are some examples I noticed while sitting at the top of a cliff looking across the Firth of Forth in Fife, Scotland:

- Walking got me to the top of the hill.
- The abseilers' gear at the top of the cliff reminded me that I could abseil down and/or climb back up it.
- A sailing boat heads towards land. It's powered by an engine but others further out to sea can be seen using their sails.
- Fishing boats also sail past.

- Clouds are taken with the wind.
- Tankers sit at the BP station with pilot boat anchored just off shore to escort it up the estuary later.
- Trains can be heard as they pass over the Forth Railway Bridge in the distance.
- Ant-like glints of cars on the new Queensferry crossing can be seen.
- Birds glide on the thermals close to the cliff.
- Kids can be seen paddling, and I'm sure will be swimming later.
- As the sailing boat nears land I realize its occupants will use the small rowing boats to get to shore from the anchor.
- Aeroplanes fly down the Forth into Edinburgh Airport.
- A seed head, perhaps a dandelion, has just wafted past, taken by the wind.
- So too a very small insect that landed on my toes momentarily, before being caught by the wind and taken away.

Other means of travelling through a landscape include:

- Paths, roads, highways, low-ways, bridges, air, water (rivers, canal or viaduct) – or none of these, just a compass in hand, or your own inner compass to guide you on your journey.
- Walking may be appropriate; however at other times you may need an elevator, bike, car, tram, train, hot air balloon, plane, glider or spaceship. What about skis, a sledge, a zip wire or horses? Other times a magic carpet might work. Or even a *Star Trek*-like transportation device (I've always dreamt of saying "Beam me up, Scottie"!)

The idea isn't that it has to work in reality, just that your mind feels it's an acceptable way of moving from the current landscape to the desired landscape. There is no right and wrong, and whatever works for you is perfect. Don't worry if you're generally quite practical, and therefore can't imagine why a magic carpet feels good to you. At some level, a part of you does know that this mode of transport is the key you needed to change the landscape.

This list may sound confusing because by giving you lots of examples, it sounds like you'll have to make lots of choices. In reality, when it comes down to answering how you're moving about the landscape you'll just know. You might not know how you know, but the answer will appear, as if from nowhere. It will appear even before you have chance to say "I don't know." Trust that the answer you get is the right one, and enjoy exploring where that takes you.

As I said, there are all manner of means of traversing the landscape. More obscure means might include being the golf ball as the golfer hits it up the fairway from the tee. Or being the ball thrown for the dog, or being a twig carried by a bird to make its nest (like in *Stick Man*, the children's book and short film).

Here are a few examples of where lines of thought can take you as you observe nature, to give you a sense of how detailed your landscapes might get – or where the solutions may come from:

I watched the meteor shower last night, sitting in the garden in my winter coat. Over the time I sat there the stars and planets in the sky "moved" position – that is, they all seemed to go clockwise from east to west. It was a reminder, of course, that we're on a planet that's rotating, with the stars relatively static, and that planets have their own orbit around the sun.

### Perhaps remembering it's the Earth that is turning would impact your landscape?

We do not physically feel the slow movement of the Earth turning every day, and yet the movement can be seen as the sun seemingly tracks from east to west and day turns to night, and the Earth generates gravity from the iron core at its centre. A gravity that we don't feel, yet which impacts our every breath.

- Perhaps imagining the core in the centre of the Earth within your landscape would change something?

- Perhaps that very act will ground your landscape in a way you've been unable to achieve thus far with other changes you've tried.

- Perhaps it's about sensing the bigger landscape within which your landscape fits – the stars, planets and galaxies above, and Earth and its molten core beneath.

- Perhaps the core of your landscape needs a little more heat or cooling.

- Perhaps the stars above need to be brighter (I'm sure I'd have seen more meteors had I been further away from the town and its street lights.)

- What would happen to your landscape if you turned off the street lights? Would the path ahead be clearer too?

- Would a meteor shower through your landscape shift the current state of stuckness?

As you can see there is no end to the solutions that may provide insight for you. It's about being observant, setting your filters and noticing what you notice about the landscape through which you're metaphorically travelling, and exploring how the characteristics you notice may be able to help your internal landscape and life.

Once you've used this technique a few times you may start to notice similarities between how you represent situations when they're working and when you're stuck. For example:

| Stuck | Unstuck |
| --- | --- |
| Black and white | Colour |
| Picture | Movie |
| Bigger than lifesize | Lifesize |
| Me in the picture | Seen through my eyes |
| No sound | Sound |
| Low sound | Louder sound |
| No temperature | Warm temperature |

Once you've identified the menu for getting unstuck, you could try it and see if it automatically enables you to access a state that helps you to find solutions to challenges you're facing.

# CONCLUSION

I trust that, as you've come on the journey with me, you've found insight for your own life. That you also now understand how the Landscaping Your Life process can continue to provide support when you notice yourself using any one of these sayings, or simply find that you're up against a brick wall and would like some help to get over, round, under it – or even to dismantle it.

The process works because we understand how nature works, perhaps more than we do our own minds. It's easier to explore a metaphorical paddle that we've lost or the creek we've found ourselves up than discuss and understand why we ended up where we have in real life.

I'd therefore encourage you to play with this process, and to have fun with it. It's certainly a tool that, in my experience over the last 20 years, many people have turned to when more conventional means have been unable to help.

The underlying premise of the book is that we all have the answers to any situation inside us – we all have our inner wisdom. Using metaphor simply allows us to find the answers wherever they're hiding inside us, and however resistant a part of us might be to following the track another part of us knows we should be headed along. In every coaching session it's this belief in our own inner knowing that enables clients using the process to obtain the insight, and have the ah-has, to enable them to get back on track. Know that I know you can do it too.

I very much look forward to hearing of your successes in using the process, and the destinations that it allows you to get to. I like to imagine readers with book in hand standing in a rut, or on a headland somewhere watching the tide, as they release whatever has been holding them back. I don't necessarily expect you to follow me to put your head in the sand... but who knows? Do send me a picture if so!

Many and enthusiastic thanks go to friends, colleagues, and workshop and coaching clients who have come on this journey with me. As new forks have appeared in the road ahead there were also people willing to come with me as we, like adventurers, explored the roads less travelled and took new (very) shiny pathways. Even if the occasional one or two turned out to be dead ends!

It was, and continues to be, about the journey and not the destination, with this book simply acting as a signpost of the journey thus far, and inspiring the journey to come.

EnJoy!

# ABOUT THE AUTHOR

Caroline Trotter

ALISON SMITH is a speaker, coach, facilitator and trainer who has developed the process of Landscaping Your Life as a method to help people get unstuck and back into their flow. She works with teams as well as individuals in business contexts and outside. Since her own personal transformation 20 years ago Alison has increasingly found the more unconventional tools to be more effective and powerful at bypassing the blocks and resistance we have to moving forward in our lives. Alison lives in Fife, Scotland.

For more information see:

**Blog:** http://alisonsmithlandscapingyourlife.blogspot.co.uk
**Website:** www.landscapingyourlife.co.uk
**Facebook:** LandscapingYourLife
**YouTube:** AlisonSmitheu/Landscaping Your Life playlist
**Pinterest:** AlisonRBCM/ Landscaping Your life board